My Dearest Sharon,
You are a Mi
Kingdom of C
A great Amba
God's Kingdom working to pull down
strongholds and everythins that exalted
itself against the kingdom of God.

Letters of
Encouragement

Proverbs 14:13 says "Every wise woman
buildeth her house: but the foolish plucketh it
down with her hands
you are a Wise woman + wife consistently
buildins up your home, church, friend,
and pourins spiritual foods into the

By

lives of Others like a runnins river.
Continue the good Works in the Lord!

Lillie M. Jenkins

Enjoy the journey with me.
God did all these wonderful and
supernatural miracles for me — He will do
the same for you and your family — Others too.

love,
Lillie Mae
March 7, 2019

xulon
PRESS

CONTENTS

                                       Page

Foreword vii

In Appreciation of Our Mother, the Author ix

Introduction xi

Book One ~ Birth of *Letters of Encouragement* 17

Book Two ~ Signs and Wonders…Do You Believe? 37

Book Three ~ *Letters of Encouragement* 59

Letter One ~ The Anointing 61

Letter Two ~ The Working of the Holy Spirit..............69
Dad, Momma and Grandma Cora

Letter Three ~ Budding—A Time for Blossoming 81

Letter Four ~ The Pecan Dream................................89

Letter Five ~ Fugitive Jonah 97

Letter Six ~ The Painful Cost of Disobedience 107

Letter Seven ~ Pray in Faith and Confidence 115

Letter Eight ~ Symptoms of a Spiritual Stroke.........123

Letter Nine ~ Petition Granted................................135

Letter Ten ~ Real Love Comes from the Heart.........145

Letter Eleven ~ The Separation—Heaven or Hell 153
Which for You?

Letter Twelve ~ Thank You, God 167

In Gratitude to Those Who Have Touched My Life 175

FOREWARD

I t is a great honor and privilege to introduce you to *Letters of Encouragement*, written by Evangelist Lillie Mae Jenkins. The author is not only an encouragement herself, but also an inspiration to all she has been blessed to meet. Having known Evangelist Jenkins for the past 13 years, I have been truly touched by her life and by the way she demonstrates her love and devotion to the well-being of humanity.

As you learn of the experiences leading up to the birth of her letters, then read those letters, I am certain you will have a new sense of hope, be strengthened and find words that lift your spirit throughout your day. The pains, struggles, joys and victories the author describes throughout her writings will give you the confidence to press forward, to endure unto the end, no matter your situation or circumstance.

The true beauty of Evangelist Jenkins' writing lies in her thoughtful intertwining of the words of Scripture with the messages of her letters. *Letters of Encouragement* will leave your heart thirsting for more words of inspiration, and Lillie Mae's devotion to the Bible will guide you to a greater appreciation for God's word. Each letter will be treasured, leaving you with a zeal to share them with others. Enjoy each letter, and be encouraged, my sister and my brothers!

Carol Reid

In Appreciation of Our Mother, the Author

A *mother's touch is what you need to survive the pressures of life. She comforts you and tells you it's okay. A mother's love can never be replaced. She sacrifices her life for you. She makes you feel better when you are down and feeling blue. She holds the family tight together like glue. Some mothers do it all by themselves...this is true. Even when you get into trouble, she never gives up on you. She prays God's protection over your life to help you get through. My, what a gift from God from Him to you!*

Never underestimate the power she has. She prays to God saying this too shall pass. Never disrespect her or take her for granted. God commanded long life. If you haven't always cherished the moments you share, one day you will be grown and Mama won't be there. Take the lessons you learned and teach your kids. It's always important to have structure. This is what Mama did. Give her the flowers while she is alive. One day her eyes will be closed and that's the final bye-bye. Remember that you only get one mother in this life. So honor, love and respect her for the rest of your life.

A mother's touch......we love our mother!

Krystal, Isaiah and Onyx

Introduction

My dear readers, I pray that as you read *Letters of Encouragement,* your life will never be the same. I trust that you will believe in your heart that, if Evangelist Jenkins survived all these storms, it is possible for you to cross over onto a safe shore.

My objective in *Letters of Encouragement* is to take you on a journey from "I can't" to "I can." In the book of Philippians, Paul encourages the Philippians that "they can" and to move forward in the strength of God. Philippians 4:13 says, *"I can do all things through Christ which strengtheneth me."*

Had it not been for God's love, grace and mercy, I would not be writing to you today. I made it. I survived the storms. You never know where God is taking you when He is silent and allows you to suffer as I have. If I would have done things my way, I would have run far away from the assignment that God entrusted to me. No one likes pain and suffering. God reminded me during those times that He was not a partial God—He loved the just and the unjust. Matthew 5:45a confirms that God is no respecter of persons, *"He maketh his sun to rise on the evil and on the good, and sendeth rain on the just and on the unjust."* Wow, that was a hard pill for me to swallow. God's answer to me for desiring to run away was found in Psalm 139: 7-9 which says, *"Whither shall I go from thy spirit? Or whither shall I flee from thy presence? If I ascend up into heaven, thou art there. If I make my bed in hell, behold, thou art there. If I take the wings of the morning, and dwell in the uttermost parts of the sea; Even then shall thy hand lead me, and thy right hand shall hold me."*

David desired to run away from all his troubles, but God said, no, you must stand and handle the pressures of life that I have placed upon you. God knew that, like David, I wanted to escape, but Psalm 55:7-8 comforts us: *"Lo, then would I wander far off, and remain in the wilderness. I would hasten my escape from the windy storm and tempest."* Yes, friends, the winds almost blew me away, but I survived and even thrived. You too can shake off the troubles besetting you. How do I know? I found by direction from the word of God in Scripture. And I am passing on those strengthening words to you in *Letters of Encouragement.*

My friends, join me on the journey of *Letters of Encouragement* and find your new life!

Evangelist Lillie Mae Jenkins

Letters of Encouragement
Write the Vision

"For the vision is yet for an appointed time, but at the end it shall speak, and not lie: though it tarry wait for it; because it will surely come, it will not tarry." Habakkuk 2:3

Chapter One

The Birth of Letters of Encouragement

Travail
Labor
Pain
Suffering

"A woman when she is in travail hath sorrow, because her hour is come: but as soon as she is delivered of the child, she remembereth no more the anguish, for joy that a man is born into the world." John 16:21

Chapter One

The Birth of "Letters of Encouragement"

Glory and honor to my Lord and Savior Jesus Christ who has brought me through much suffering and pain in giving birth to *Letters of Encouragement*.

In 2002, I returned to New York City, where I had spent most of my adult life, to be granted a license as a Gospel Evangelist in the first step of my journey in Christian counseling. It was there that a divine prophetic word was spoken into my spirit as I sat in the home of Pastor Joe L. Brown and his lovely wife, Laura Brown. I had enjoyed the opportunity of serving under their leadership as Deaconess, choir member and President of the Welcome Committee. I enjoyed knowing them, along with Pastor Brown's sister, Pastor Mary Jo Young, for more than twenty-four years.

The divine word came from Pastor Joe L. Brown who presented me with a question: "Now that you are an Evangelist, what are you going to do?" I told him that I would preach the gospel, to which he responded, "There is more to the gospel than preaching. Write a book." When I questioned this directive, Pastor Joe L. Brown continued, "God has given you a writing epistle ministry, and you have written countless letters to people throughout the church." He advised me to title the book *"Letters of Encouragement."* I sensed from his words that my wonderful pastor was directing me to share my love of scripture. He was telling me to use my knowledge of scripture to show others how the answers to life's problems can be found in the words of the Bible.

I told Pastor Joe L. Brown that I would ask God for guidance. Upon returning to South Carolina, I began praying to God, asking Him if I was capable of undertaking the responsibility of such a task. God's answer was a compelling "Yes", but the confirmation of His message came to me only much later, in the form of a supernatural, angelic visitation in my home, which I shall share with you shortly.

****

My testimony of *Letters of Encouragement* will come as a surprise, even a shock, to many of you, my wonderful friends and dear readers. It is by the grace of God that this book has come to be born.

God answered my prayers with that compelling "Yes", but my reaction was as though a levy had broken loose into my life. The impact of the spiritual waters rushing through that broken levy was so strong that I began to suffer tremendous assaults, spiritually, emotionally and physically—a demonic attack.

I began questioning my own faith in God. Doubts set in. Even though I knew that He died on the cross for me, I wondered if God loved me. I felt as though life was not worth living. I experienced moments of deep despair. My only hope was to sleep away and never waken to the dawning of a new day. Instead, I suffered countless nights without sleep, was anxious and severely fatigued. As long as I was mobile I was surviving, but the moment I rested, I became a zombie.

Only then could I drift into a deep sleep, my head bowed down to my chest.

I was miserable and hated to see nightfall. I called my bed the "hell bed." The more I tried to sleep, the more my bed seemed to spin around my bedroom. During my travels to the bathroom at night I walked holding onto the walls. Even the simple task of washing dishes required me to place a chair at the sink so I could sit if I lost my balance. My head felt as though I was on a roller coaster ride. I was nauseous, breaking out in hot sweats, my head swimming. I was so exhausted that I desperately asked God to let me die.

I was even at the point of running from health food shops to local pharmacies trying to find something that would relieve my depression. I spent huge amounts of money on energy liquids and energy-boosting vitamin pills, none of them relieving my suffering. The frustration and discouragement, along with non-stop physical pain, finally forced me to get myself to the hospital late one night. Upon explaining my symptoms to the doctor, he recommended that I pay a visit to the Department of Psychiatry. "The Devil is a liar!" I declared. "I am in my right mind, I am not going anywhere." It was then that I began to realize that I was actually in a spiritual battle which was not from a natural perspective— it was something from the pits of hell that the Devil had released upon my body and mind. That night I began to fight back against the attacks. And with that, God gave me new strength to persevere.

******

During this time of trial, my countenance was one of a jubilant and vibrant mother, encourager, company receptionist, Sunday school teacher and evangelist. On the inside, however, I was miserable. Many days I cried in my car as I drove to and from the mall, my work, my church and various other places. Many tears were shed at my desk, but thankfully, no one ever saw. I wore two faces and lived two different lives. I wore a happy face from 8 a.m. to 5:00 p.m. But as I left work, the face of my depression re-appeared. I wore a clown's mask for years. As you, my dear friends, read this you may be surprised, but please allow me to be truthful. Confession is good for the soul. And, in spite of my two faces, God kept me.

I stayed under prayer and fasting. There were times when I fasted for seven, twenty-one, even sixty days, as well as many other times, so that when you came to me for prayer and encouragement, I was ready and able to get a prayer of healing through to God for you—and God healed many of you.

During this dreadful time, God kept my countenance bright and beautiful. There were no signs of my sadness. Through all of this I did not let my God or my guard down. I morally lived what I ministered to you. There were times that I shared my sufferings privately with my pastor, but every time I entered the doors for church service, I did so with a radiant smile. No one had the slightest notion that I had spent the previous night moaning in pain. There were times that I asked God to release me from life. Yet I prayed, "God, just let me get to the house of prayer once more, please Lord." I knew that if I could make it into the house of prayer, I could make it through the next night. I truly believed that once I walked through those doors, God's prophetic word awaited me.

During one such visit to the house of prayer, I was anxious and eager for the servant of God, Pastor William Prioleau, to come forth with a word preached from the Lord. As if in answer to my petitions, God spoke to the pastor, sharing in spirit all that I had endured the nights and weeks before. It seemed that God had given him a spiritual crystal ball enabling him to reveal to me the inner being of all my anger, anxious thoughts and pains. Pastor preached to my soul and my soul was gleeful. His words spoke to my heart: "Stop getting mad with God, stop blaming God—blame the Devil, don't give up, don't lose your focus." This simple, yet powerful message exposed to me the source of my frustration and my pain. And this message carried me forward, giving me strength, day by day. Thank you, Pastor William Prioleau!

My daughter Krystal and my friend Kellie also knew what I had been enduring. I confessed to them that at times I felt as though I was lying on my death bed, just waiting to exhale my last breath. But these dear ladies were like fuel pumps. They kept pumping energy into my spirit with words of support: "Don't you give up, hang in there, the devil wants you to give up—your breakthrough is on the way." Thank you, Krystal and Kellie!

****

During these years of distress and agony, I had not forgotten Pastor Joe L. Brown's directive to write my book, but I also knew that I must heed my calling as an evangelist. I realized that I needed a formal religious education, so I enrolled in a Christian bible college where I earned a bachelors degree in Bible Studies in 2004 and immediately began courses for a masters degree in Christian Counseling.

Finally, in 2006, I took what I thought would be the first steps to actually composing my book. On the night of September 26, I felt driven to make several signs and to post them about my house to reinforce the messages my soul was expressing.

On three full-size sheets of paper the following was written: *"Write your book within ten days 9/26/2006"*, *"Sixty days of fasting and praying, supernatural miracles, wholesome mate, financial blessings, and healings"* and

"Write the vision". Using red ink, I imprinted four more signs several times with a personalized stamp I had made. It said simply, "I'm a Millionaire." When I had finished all seven signs, I used tape to post them throughout my house: on doorposts outside of my bedroom, computer room, living room, kitchen, even my refrigerator doors.

I fully expected that, with a burst of enthusiasm, I would immediately be inspired to start writing. But no inspiration came to me, only disappointment and frustration. Finally, one afternoon in October, 2006, I came home from work, walked around my house and read each of the posted signs. Then with a vengeance, I tore down ALL of the signs and threw them in the kitchen garbage can. I declared out loud, "This is not going to happen!" And with that, I put the kitchen garbage bag into the large trash bin and placed the bin outside on the curb for the next morning's trash pick-up. This, my friends, would have been the end of my mission to write *Letters of Encouragement*, but God had other plans for me.

One month later, on a morning in November, I woke at 6:00 a.m. as usual in preparation for work. In my normal routine, I turned on a light in the living room. It was then that I witnessed God's mandate to me. I glanced up and saw one of the signs taped to the living room doorpost. Looking around the house, I realized that EVERY SIGN that I had thrown in the garbage was posted back in its original spot! But one of the signs was in a different location. The one that read

Write my book within 10 days
Everynite
9/26/2006

was now posted on the kitchen door leading outside. The sign was just above the door knob so that I had to see it as I left the house. Astonished at the sight, I screamed in amazement! Then I realized that the original pieces of tape used to post the signs were still attached to them. And the signs were marked with GREASE STAINS, proving to me that they were, in fact, the signs I had thrown in the trash in October! (Please see the signs nearby.)

This angelic visitation was my confirmation, authorized by God, that *Letters of Encouragement* must be written and published. I knew that I could not escape the mandate that God now made visible to my eyes. I am writing solemn truth. This is not a fairytale story. All that I have written to you is nothing but truthful and factual. I personally experienced all that I have said to you. And I trust that after reading this story of my journey, you too will believe that you can and will move forward in the prophecy that God has mandated for your life.

******

Despite this confirmation of God's compelling answer of "Yes" to my first prayers, I did not actually begin to write my book until March 2009. Having finally earned the masters degree in Christian Counseling that February, I was now ready and quite anxious to compose *Letters of Encouragement*. Allow me to share with you that the writing has been easy for me—but the suffering preceding that writing was phenomenal. All I have done is sit at the computer and record everything that God has given me to minister to you. I had many doubtful moments when I questioned that I would survive the attacks that plagued me for so many years, but I travailed as one giving birth to a child as I wrote these words to you.

Friends, God can do the impossible. He has the power to deliver you and to set you free. I hope that in some way *Letters of Encouragement* will inspire you in the vision that God has called you to. My prayer is that, as you continue to read *Letters of Encouragement,* the intensity of your faith will grow.

I recall Evangelist Ena Prioleau's message: "Salvation is free, but the anointing is a cost." How well do I now know this to be true. Thank you, Evangelist!

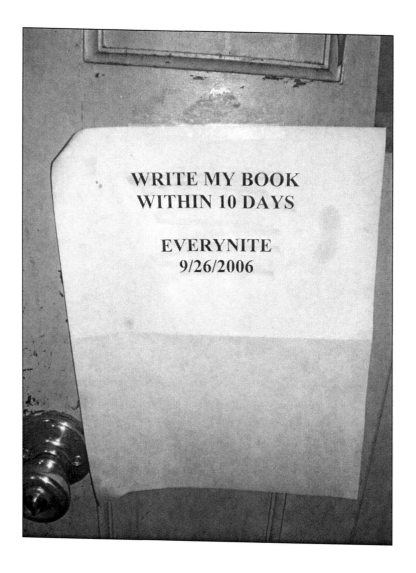

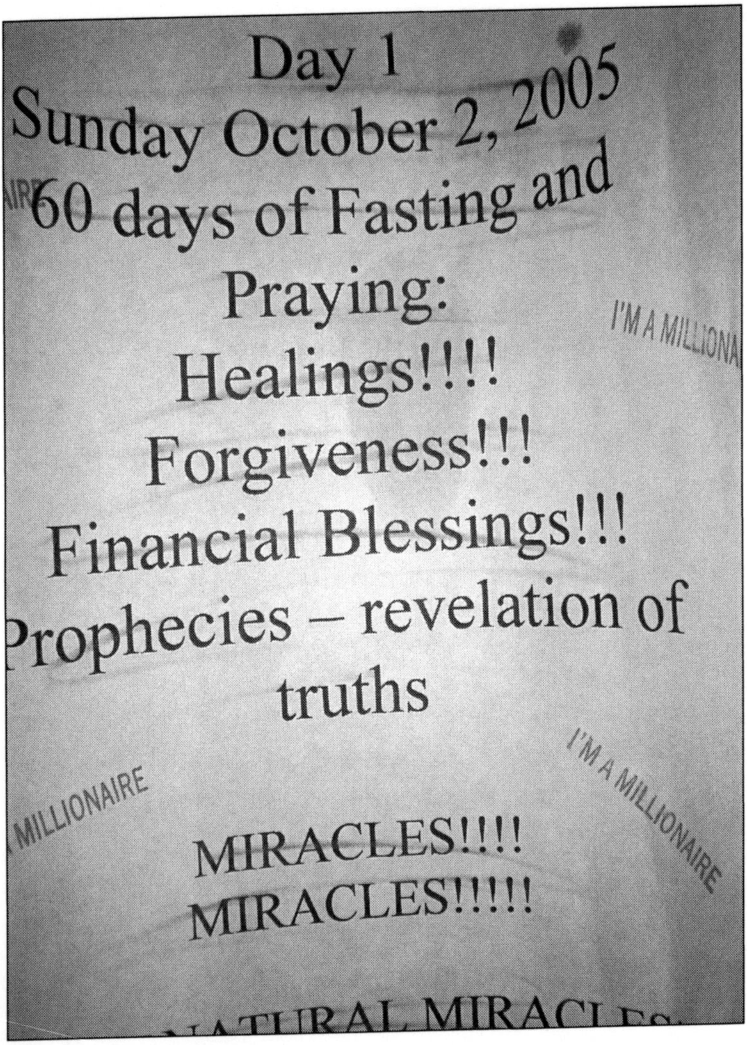

Day 1
Sunday October 2, 2005
60 days of Fasting and
Praying:
Healings!!!!
Forgiveness!!!
Financial Blessings!!!
Prophecies – revelation of
truths

I'M A MILLIONAIRE

MILLIONAIRE

MIRACLES!!!!
MIRACLES!!!!!

NATURAL MIRACLES

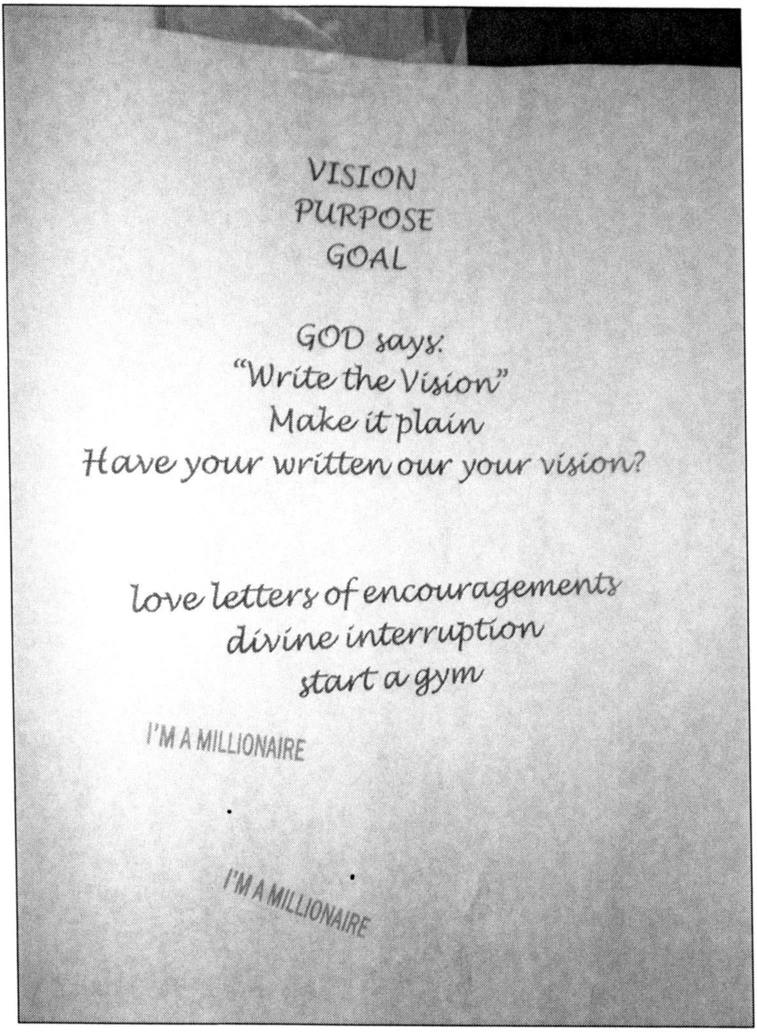

VISION
PURPOSE
GOAL

GOD *says*:
"Write the Vision"
Make it plain
Have your written our your vision?

love letters of encouragements
divine interruption
start a gym

I'M A MILLIONAIRE

I'M A MILLIONAIRE

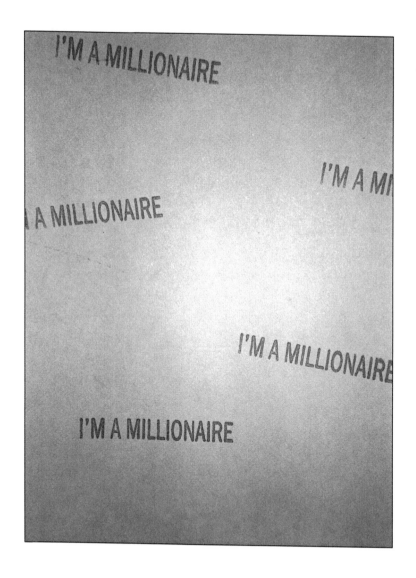

FROM THE DESK OF
LILLIE MAE JENKINS

I'M A MILLIONAIRE

I'M A MILLIONAIRE

I'M A MILLIONAIRE

I'M A M

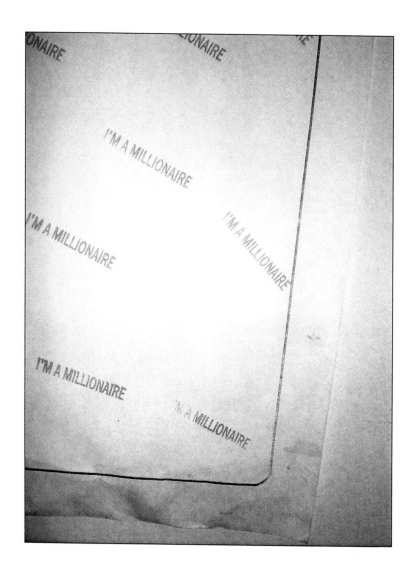

Chapter Two

Signs and Wonders...
Do You Believe?

"And it shall come to pass in the last days, saith God, I will pour out of my Spirit upon all flesh: and your sons and your daughters shall prophesy, and your young men shall see visions, and your old men shall dream dreams." Acts 2:17

Chapter Two

Signs and Wonders...
Do you believe?

A fter reading about the birth of *Letters of Encouragement*, I trust that you will believe in *Signs and Wonders*. The Bible is filled with many of God's prophetic promises, visions, angelic visitations, and countless miracles. Joel 2:28-29 states: *"And it shall come to pass afterward, that I will pour out my spirit upon all flesh; and your sons and your daughters shall prophesy, your old men shall dream dreams, your young men shall see visions: And also upon the servants and upon the handmaids in those days will I pour out my spirit."*

Here, we find Joel prophesying that an outpouring of God's spirit will fall upon anyone who makes himself available to God, and anyone can witness the awesomeness of what the spirit of God will bring to pass in their life. In other words, if you are in the right place with God (living a clean spiritual life), you can experience the same supernatural miracles as I have. To capture this experience, you must have faith and believe that the miracles God performed over two thousand years ago He is quite capable of performing in your life today. According to Hebrews 11:6, *"But without faith it is impossible to please him: for he that cometh to God must believe that he is, and that he is a rewarder of them that diligently seek him."* And then, Hebrews 13:8 says, *"Jesus Christ the same yesterday, and today, and for ever."* Pay close attention to what the word of God is saying. Believe— if God healed you years ago, why not believe that He is powerful enough to heal you today? Friends, it is your faith that will prompt God to work on your behalf.

****

Having a sincere relationship with God and being in good standing with Him brings great blessings upon your life. Let's read the miracle of Zechariah and Elisabeth concerning the birth of their son John the Baptist. Zechariah experienced a visit by the angel of the Lord. Luke 1:6-13 states: *"And they were both righteous before God, walking in all the commandments and ordinances of the Lord blameless. And they had no child, because that Elisabeth was barren, and they both were now well stricken in years. And it came to pass, that while he executed the priest's office before God in the order of his course, According to the custom of the priest's office, his lot was to burn incense when he went into the temple of the Lord. And the whole multitude of the people were praying without at the time of incense. And there appeared unto him an angel of the Lord standing on the right side of the altar of incense. And when Zechariah saw him, he was troubled, and fear fell upon him. But the angel said unto him, Fear not, Zechariah: for thy prayer is heard; and thy wife Elisabeth shall bear thee a son, and thou shalt call his name John."* According to Luke 1:18-20, Zechariah doubted the prophecy spoken by the angel sent by God. *"And Zechariah said unto the angel, Whereby shall I know this? For I am an old man, and my wife well stricken in years. And the angel answering said unto him, I am Gabriel, that stand in the presence of God; and am sent to speak unto thee, and to show thee these glad tidings. And, behold, thou shalt be dumb, and not able to speak, until the day that these things shall be performed, because thou believest not my words, which shall be fulfilled in their season."*

My dear friends, as is revealed in all that is stated above, failure to believe blocks blessings. You must believe! The mouth of Zechariah was made silent. Why? He doubted. In the natural, can we say that a bridle was placed upon Zechariah's mouth as upon a horse's mouth until the birth of his son?

****

I direct your attention to another angelic visitation—the Lion's Den. Daniel, Hananiah, Mishael and Azariah, were of the children of Judah (see Daniel 1:6). They were taken into captivity by Nebuchadnezzar, King of Babylon (see Daniel 1:1). Daniel 1:17 states: *"As for these four children, God gave them knowledge and skill in all learning and wisdom: and Daniel had understanding in all visions and dreams."* The scripture says: *"Nebuchadnezzar the king made an image of gold, whose height was threescore cubits, and the breadth thereof six cubits: he set it up in the plain of Dura, in the province of Babylon."* (Daniel 3:1) After making the golden image, Nebuchadnezzar gathered all people that were under his governorship. He then decreed that, at what time the people hear all kinds of music, they were to fall down and worship the golden image (see Daniel 3:2-6).

According to Daniel 3:12a, a report was taken back to the king. The scripture states: *"Shadrach, Meshach and Abednego; these men, O king, have not regarded thee: they serve not thy gods, nor worship the golden image which thou hast set up."* Nebuchadnezzar spoke personally with the three men, trying to persuade them a second time to bow

43

down to his golden image. Again, they refused (see Daniel 3:15-18). *"Then was Nebuchadnezzar full of fury, and the form of his visage was changed against Shadrach, Meshach and Abednego: therefore he spake, and commanded that they should heat the furnace one seven times more than it was wont to be heated."* (Daniel 3:19)

The three men were full of faith. They were ready to be thrown into the furnace by Nebuchadnezzar. They knew the power and strength of their God, assured that He would deliver them. Why? They were believers in miracles. Friends, read along with me the story of their supernatural, angelic deliverance. Daniel 3:20-26 says, *"And he commanded the most mighty men that were in his army to bind Shadrach, Meshach, and Abednego, and to cast them into the burning fiery furnace. Then these men were bound in their coats, their hosen, and their hats, and their other garments, and were cast into the midst of the burning fiery furnace. Therefore because the king's commandment was urgent, and the furnace exceeding hot, the flame of the fire slew those men that took up Shadrach, Meshach, and Abednego. And these three men, Shadrach, Meshach, and Abednego, fell down bound into the midst of the burning fiery furnace. Then Nebuchadnezzar the king was astonished, and rose up in haste, and spake, and said unto his counselors, Did not we cast three men bound into the midst of the fire? They answered and said unto the king, True, O king. He answered and said, Lo, I see four men loose, walking in the midst of the fire, and they have no hurt; and the form of the fourth is like the Son of God. Then Nebuchadnezzar came near to the mouth of the burning fiery furnace, and spake, and said, Shadrach, Meshach, and Abednego, ye servants of the most high God, come forth, and come hither. Then Shadrach, Meshach, and Abednego, came forth of the midst of the fire."* Verse 23 states that three men were thrown into the fiery furnace. Verse 25 confirms a divine intercession—four men loose, walking in the midst of the fire.

At this point, I suspect that you may believe in miracles. God can deliver you out of any and every situation. He will send an angel to guard you, to lift you up. He stands ready to deliver you in the day of trouble. God said to Jeremiah: *"Behold, I am the LORD, the God of all flesh: is there any thing too hard for me?"* (Jeremiah 32:27)

****

Please allow me to share with you a few of my own supernatural, angelic experiences of *Signs and Wonders*.

My first encounter with the signs and wonders of God occurred in 1989 at my home in New York City. I had previously stored away in our overcrowded attic our most important papers in a large gold envelope: our marriage license, birth certificates, graduation diplomas, death certificates, baptismal papers, and retirement letters. One day I was thinking about one of the papers in the envelope, and it was then that I realized that I had forgotten where in the attic I had stored the envelope. For months I frantically searched and prayed, beseeching God to give me a vision of the envelope's location.

After months with no results, on a Sunday afternoon my family and I attended an evening program at church. We returned home around 7:30 p.m., and my husband went to bed early. The children were in their rooms watching TV, so I had some private time to again search for the gold envelope.

I came to the bedroom, fell down on bended knees and pleaded, "God, this is my last prayer. I am not going to bother you anymore after tonight, so please show me where those papers are." After praying with a sincere heart, I rose and looked to my left where I spotted a large gold envelope—the same gold envelope that I had been searching for so desperately. I cried out in shock, but my husband was not awakened by my scream. I ran to my children's bedrooms describing what had just occurred. I then showed them the envelope that I discovered lying on the floor by the foot of the bed. They believed. Why? Because both were eyewitnesses to my daily living and prayer life, alone and together.

Later that evening, I called Lizelle. I recounted all that had transpired, and she too believed. She knew the power of prayer for she was a prayer warrior.

The following Wednesday night I attended choir rehearsal. I asked permission to give testimony of this supernatural occurrence when the rehearsal ended. I shared with the others all that had transpired leading up to the miracle of my discovery. The people had mixed reactions: some believed while others were quiet and said nothing. One choir member challenged, "Are you sure you did not put the envelope there and then forgot that it was there?" I left rehearsal that night disappointed because some of the people had doubted and did not believe in *Signs and Wonders*. From that night on, it was clear in my mind that I would never share an experience openly again but only with those to whom God would direct me. Friends, remember that not everyone will accept or understand your vision. There are times you must find yourself in quiet and stillness before the Lord. The truth will eventually manifest itself to others.

Today, I am in fullness of understanding of why God allowed this miracle to happen in 1989. According to Esther 4:14, it was *"for such a time as this?"* God gave me a good teaching lesson. Paul states in Romans 11:33: *"O the depth of the riches both of the wisdom and knowledge of God! How unsearchable are his judgments, and his ways past finding out!"* Dear readers, God is powerful and His strength is deep. Do not try to comprehend His infinite wisdom. Pastor William Prioleau consistently reminded the people, "Stop trying to figure out God: His ways are deep." Goodness, what an awesome man of God, full of knowledge and wisdom.

****

As time passed following this experience, my relationship with God waxed stronger. He began to speak to me in dreams. I had numerous visions of myself preaching in the pulpit. This continued for at least eight years when, finally, God confirmed to me that He had placed a call upon my life to preach the gospel of Christ.

At times during those years, however, my dreams went in a different direction. I began to have dreams of friends and loved ones passing away. Amazingly, within days the events in the dreams actually happened.

God worked in other ways in my life. If, at my job, someone mistreated me or took advantage of me, God would move them into a new job. On one occasion, an adversary of mine came to work and out of the clear blue announced, "I am quitting." I Chronicles 16:21-22 states: *"He suffered no man to do them wrong: yea, he reproved kings for their sakes, Saying, Touch not mine anointed, and do my prophets no harm."* We must be very careful with respect to God's servants if they have not harmed us. Leave them alone! You do not want the wrath of God to retaliate against you.

****

Many angelic events occurred in my life. There were several times that, just like the large gold envelope, misplaced items were brought back to me. If I left an item in a particular place and then could not find it for days, months or even longer, it was placed in an open location in my presence.

I remember the day after Christmas one year, I purchased two identical birthstone rings. Leaving work for home on a

Friday, I had driven about five miles when I discovered that I had left both rings at work. One of my tasks was opening all incoming mail. I used gloves to prevent hand dryness, so I removed the birthstone rings to put on the gloves. But I forgot to put the rings back on before leaving. The entire weekend, I kept touching my ring finger out of habit, remembering that I had left the rings on my desk. But, are you ready for the angelic visitation? As I was dressing for church on Sunday morning, I returned to my bedroom to put on my jewelry. There, on my dresser, were both of the rings! Once again, I screamed and praised God.

Dear friends, I have enough miracles to share with you for the rest of my life, but please allow me to recount the occurrence of just one more event. My husband, Howard, passed in 1999, but I never expected to re-marry. On April 26, 2009, I attended a Sunday morning church service. Pastor William Prioleau's theme was "Waiting on God," and his message directed listeners to be patient, not to go in search of a husband or wife; that God will bring a spouse from across the river, from another place. Sunday evening, another speaker again addressed the theme of endurance, "Waiting on God."

My routine on weekends is to launder my clothes on Saturday, then place them on my living room sofa for air drying. When I returned home from church that Sunday evening, I unlocked the back door, entered the kitchen and then went into the living room, whereupon the Lord immediately said to me, "Fold your clothes." I began folding the clothes with only a light on in the kitchen. As I lifted the pieces of clothing from the sofa, however, I realized that one item was heavier than the others. I knew it was not something I had washed and, standing in near darkness, I questioned what it was.

I turned on the light as I carried the item into the bedroom. Friends, are you ready? The item I was holding was a powder-blue tee shirt, embossed with silver beads which spelled the word "bride." I screamed in wonder! I had not seen this shirt in THREE YEARS! It was given to me by my friend Candace, a skillful and creative person whose talent was making beautiful gifts. I had not washed this tee shirt with the other items, yet I found it lying there with the clothes on the sofa. The lesson I took from that day's sermons and the mysterious appearance of the shirt was that God has a plan for us. We must "wait on God," because He will do wondrous things for us, but only in His time. Nonetheless, we can listen to messages and take note of signs along the way as we wait patiently for God to reveal His plan. (Please see photo of "bride" shirt nearby.)

****

I spoke earlier of the physical and emotional reaction I had to God's mandate in 2002 that I write *Letters of Encouragement*. But prior to that period in my life, another supernatural miracle was visited upon me. In October of 2001, I became quite ill. I was constantly fatigued, nauseous, had no appetite and was jaundiced in both eyes. I made several visits to my personal physician. His staff performed complete blood work which was sent out to the lab for testing. Despite two lab tests coming back as negative, I continued to suffer. The doctor had decided not to write any prescriptions until he could draw conclusions from the test results.

After two weeks with no improvement and feeling worse than I did on my initial visit, I returned to the doctor's office on a Friday morning around 8:30 a.m. and requested a test for cancer. Thinking along the same line, the doctor immediately scheduled a CT scan for that same day. I returned back to his office that afternoon at approximately 1:30 p.m. when he informed me that I had a mass on the left lobe of my liver which was causing me to feel so sick. After that statement I said nothing. I returned home that weekend and, from Friday to Sunday, I read the bible and prayed. I was too sick to eat anything. I told only a handful of family members about my condition and got word to Pastor William Priouleau and his wife Ena. They were attending the National Convention in Memphis, but they took time out of their worship to call me with a list of healing scriptures to read out loud. I was so grateful for their kindness and concern.

During this time of illness, the Lord instructed me to read Second Kings, Chapter 20, which described Hezekiah's sickness and recovery. Friends, please read along with me. 2 Kings 20:7 says, *"And Isaiah said, Take a lump of figs. And they took and laid it on the boil, and he recovered."* After reading this passage, I went to my sister-in-law's mother's house in search of a fig tree. Bless God! A fig tree was in her mother's yard, but there were no figs on the tree, only leaves. I took several leaves, brought them home, wrapped them in aluminum foil and placed the packet on my bosom where I kept it from Friday to Sunday. I continued reading and praying in scriptures. On the third day, Sunday morning, the Lord woke me around 5:30 a.m. These are the words God said to me: "I have healed your body, and not only have I healed you, but I have also cured a family member. This relative was healed of a rare disease." I jumped up and began praising God. I called my sister-in-law to proclaim that God had healed my body, and she cried. She had gone with me to the doctor and knew how sick I was. She then declared: "I can hear healing in your voice."

Sunday morning I drank a cup of orange juice and ate a very large turkey sandwich. I had not been able to eat for weeks, and goodness, that sandwich was delicious! My appetite had returned and the sensation of sickness had completely left my body. I went to church that Sunday morning and testified that I was healed.

But there is a second part of this miracle: that same day, Friday, November 2, 2001, when the doctor had given me the results of the CT scan, he ordered a second test, this time an MRI.

Friends, guess what? The doctor never called me with the results of the MRI which was done on November 16, 2001. I then shared with my family that I was not going back to the doctor's office for two reasons. First, I had not heard from him. Second, I knew that my body was healed and there was no reason for my return.

However, my family insisted that I move forward in making a revisit appointment. They felt that it was necessary for the doctor to be the one to confirm my healing. So, I called the doctor's office for a second appointment.

Two weeks later, Monday, November 26, 2001, I met with the doctor just to prove to my family that I was healed. That morning, while preparing for my appointment, God spoke these specific words into my spirit: "Read John 11:4." This Scripture passage states that, *"This sickness is not unto death, but for the glory of God, that the Son of God might be glorified thereby."*

After reading this, I journeyed to the doctor's office. Shortly thereafter I was called in by the nurse. When we met, the doctor asked what he could do for me. I first responded, "Doctor, do you believe in miracles?" He stated that he did. I then said to him, "I don't know what the MRI test results are, but the third day after the CT scan indicated a spot on my liver, God healed my body as I lay asleep." The doctor then stated, "Well, your MRI showed that there is NO CANCER IN YOUR LIVER OR ANYWHERE IN YOUR BODY." I cried out, "I told you, I told you!" The nurse and staff came out of their offices proclaiming that they believed in miracles as well. I did not have any idea why God told me to read John 11:4, but I followed His word. Little did I know that this scripture was my "healing confirmation." Dear readers,

I believe in biblical fig tree healing. If you have been diagnosed with sickness or disease, I challenge you to believe— go for it! God healed me and He will heal you. (Please see diagnosis nearby.)

So, my friends, are you ready to hear about another supernatural miracle? In 2004, I was diagnosed with Renal Kidney Disease, but I was never informed of the diagnosis. A year later, 2005, I received a letter from the hospital stating that I needed to see a physician within two to three weeks for a blood test. It was at this visit that I asked the doctor to compare the results of the 2004 and 2005 tests. While the doctor was viewing my earlier records, I saw the words "Renal Disease."

I was shocked and asked why no one had contacted me about my diagnosis of renal disease a year earlier. I was furious and said I was going to pursue action. I insisted on further testing to determine if the disease had progressed since my blood test in 2004.

The doctor immediately ordered a sonogram of my kidneys which was conducted two days later, on a Friday. Between the day the doctor ordered the sonogram and the day of the procedure, I fervently prayed, beseeching God to please give me another chance to eat right and to please heal my body.

That Friday, the day of the sonogram, this is what took place as I lay on table. The radiologist was moving a ball-like instrument back and forth on top of my abdomen. She said, "There's nothing wrong with your bladder. And look over here, look over there, your kidneys are fine. What are you doing here?" I screamed and said thank you Jesus!

Throughout *Signs and Wonders*, I have called you my friends. Why? I believe that we have now gained confidence in each other and that you are a believer of supernatural miracles as I am. My prayer for you today is that God will open your eyes and reveal Himself to you in a supernatural way. Believe that God can do anything but fail. These miracles have actually taken place. There is nothing that I have written to you that I have not experienced. And I hope that you can find inspiration for God's purpose in your life in my *Letters of Encouragement*.

Hospital Diagnostics

Name: JENKINS,LILLIE MAE   MR#:
Exam Date: 11/16/01   DOB:
Ord. Phy.:   Pt. Phone#:
                                             Ord. Phy.#:
                                             Phy. Fax #:

                                             Acct_Nbr
                                             Pat_Type

Chk-in #   Order   Exam
                         FMR ABDOMEN W/WO CONTRAST MRI
                            Ord Diag: LIVER MASS

MRI OF THE ABDOMEN WITH ATTENTION TO THE LIVER, 11-16-01:

COMPARISON: Report from   Medical   ultrasound,
11-9-01.

The patient has a history of nausea, weakness, and fatigue, and a
mass seen on the liver on previous ultrasound.

T1 and T2 weighted axial images were obtained followed by serial
post-gadolinium images in varying phases of enhancement, followed by
coronal post-gadolinium images.

Several lesions are seen throughout the liver with characteristics
consistent with benign simple cysts. These include at least two 1
cm oval lesions in the left lobe of the liver consistent with benign
simple cysts. A 3 by 2 cm area of abnormal signal is seen at the
anterior margin of the junction of right and left hepatic lobes,
extending superiorly through the right cardiophrenic sulcus. It is
difficult to tell if this lies above or beneath the right
hemidiaphragm, but does not appear to lie within the liver. It has
unusual signal characteristics, with increasing on both T1 and T2
weighted images. Otherwise no sign of the mass is seen in the
region of the liver. Spleen, adrenals, pancreas, and kidneys are
unremarkable. No adenopathy is seen. No ascites is noted.

IMPRESSION:

Several small benign cysts are seen within the liver, some of which
are in the left lobe measuring about a cm. The lesion seen on
ultrasound is described as solid. There is an unusual 3 by 2 cm
curvilinear type density anterior to the liver and extending into
the right cardiophrenic sulcus. It is difficult to tell if this
lies within the chest or within the abdomen. CT would be useful to
further characterize this lesion, and evaluate for the possibility
FINAL DUPLICATE
- -
                        Hospital Imaging Services

57

Chapter Three

Letters of Encouragement

"And David was greatly distressed; for the people spake of stoning him, because the soul of all the people was grieved, every man for his sons and for his daughters: but David encouraged himself in the LORD his God." I Samuel 30:6

Letter One

The Anointing

"*And Moses took the anointing oil, and anointed the tabernacle and all that was therein, and sanctified them. And he sprinkled thereof upon the altar seven times, and anointed the altar and all his vessels, both the laver and his foot, to sanctify them. And he poured of the anointing oil upon Aaron's head, and anointed him, to sanctify him.*"
Leviticus 8:10-12

Letter One

The Anointing

A fter receiving Christ as my personal Lord and Savior, I longed for a more intimate relationship with Him, and I found myself engaged in daily reading and praying. I yearned to cross over into higher heights and deeper depths. I felt a pull from God as though I was being pulled by a huge tug boat. That was the Holy Ghost's power resting and operating within me. Without His power, I would have no strength to sustain the challenges of life's strong winds and storms. The strength of God kept me from being blown away. I avoided going in an ill-fated direction and stayed surrounded by the will of God. I knew that choosing and having God as the center piece of my heart would take me directly into the holiest of holies. It is a secret place of the High God. I fought and stood the test of trying to keep my life in right standing with God. When the time was right, I would be ready to enter, wherein my life would never be the same again. Today, I can truthfully say that, with this precious gift living inside me, I have been enabled to stand the trials and injustices of life.

The secret dwelling is the most intimate place to be when it comes to having a closer relationship with God. This is where you will find yourself soaking in God's presence and glory. The anointing of God is very powerful. It envelopes, hides and conceals as a mantle that covers head to toe. Have you ever had an experience of this magnitude?

My dear readers, may I share with you the effects of the glory: the anointing by God when it fell upon King Solomon's followers and all congregations of Israel in the holy temple into which the ark of God was brought? According to I Kings 8:6-11: *"And the priests brought in the ark of the covenant of the Lord unto his place, into the oracle of the house, to the most holy place, even under the wings of the cherubim. For the cherubim spread forth their two wings over the place of the ark, and the cherubim covered the ark and the staves thereof above. And they drew out the staves, that the ends of the staves were seen out in the holy place before the oracle, and they were not seen without: and there they are unto this day. There was nothing in the ark save the two tables of stone, which Moses put there at Horeb, when the Lord made a covenant with the children of Israel, when they came out of the land of Egypt. And it came to pass, when the priests were come out of the holy place, that the cloud filled the house of the Lord. So that the priests could not stand to minister because of the cloud: for the glory of the Lord had filled the house of the Lord."*

Today, you too can enter into the holy place by going directly to God, into His holy temple, just as Solomon's followers did. You may not fully understand the anointing power of God, but I can assure you that if you make yourself available, God will reveal Himself to you in His fullness. Psalm confirms, *"Thou wilt show me the path of life: in thy presence is fullness of joy; at thy right hand there are pleasures for evermore."* (Psalm 16:11)

If you desire to have the anointing power of God resting upon your life, seek God. Matthew 6:33 tells us, *"But seek ye first the kingdom of God, and his righteousness; and all these things shall be added unto you."* Then Matthew 7:7-8 says, *"Ask, and it shall be given you; seek, and ye shall find; knock, and it shall be opened unto you: For every one that asketh receiveth; and he that seeketh findeth; and to him that knocketh it shall be opened."*

May I close in leaving you with a question? Are you thirsty and hungry for the living God?

Letter Two

The Working of the Holy Spirit
Dad, Mom and Grandma Cora

"Honor thy father and thy mother: that thy days may be long upon the land which the LORD thy God giveth thee." Exodus 20:12

Letter Two

The Working of the Holy Spirit
Dad, Momma and Grandma Cora

T he *Working of the Holy Spirit* is in memory of three wonderful people who instilled so much into my life. As a child and throughout my adolescent years, I was raised in church, and I had the wonderful opportunity of witnessing the effects of the power of God in the lives of my parents and my grandmother, Cora. There was no doubt that the Spirit of God rested upon them.

Dad was a deacon, and he sang in the choir. He never had the chance to attend school. Instead, he devoted his "school days" to the needs of his parents, sisters and brothers, nineteen of them.

Despite his lack of education, Daddy was a master of the trades, a plumber and carpenter. He even added an extra bedroom onto our first home. Dad was also a great help to the community. He did many free plumbing jobs and was always repairing things for neighbors. I remember him returning home many times smeared in dirt and grease from working under houses and in deep holes.

Daddy was also a cosmetologist. When I was a little girl, my father braided and permed my hair and did so for my sisters Dorothy and Debra as well. Willie Mae and Gloria had natural-born curly hair, so they did not need a perm, nor did my brothers, James and Charles, who had such nice hair. Back in the fifties, permed hair was called "processed hair." An iron comb made with a wooden handle and steel teeth was used, and lard, a creamy white soft substance used for cooking, was applied to the hair as grease straightener. Daddy was our personal hair stylist!

My father was an excellent provider who took good care of his family. Not only did he support us well, but he loved and cared for us, allowing no one to mistreat us. I recall on several occasions that Daddy had to pull out his rifle to remind a few folks just who his children really belonged to. On paydays Daddy came directly home and gave his pay check to our mother instead of cashing it and squandering the money. And I never saw my father running the street with other women to my mother's face.

Cooking was another of my father's skills, especially when it came to the sweet homemade cakes that he baked on Sundays. And Daddy was a very competent hunter, bringing home deer, rabbit, squirrel and possum. To this day, I pause for a moment in laughter recalling Daddy's baked possum with sweet potato on the side. In those days, these were delicacies! And the most magnificent memory of my childhood was seeing my daddy many, many times kneeling in the kitchen and praying in front of the stove. The kitchen was his sanctuary where he met God in prayer.

Daddy was not a perfect man, but he was a good man. Momma loved Daddy regardless of the situation. They stayed married unto death for forty years. Back in the olden days, marriage was held to be very sacred and dear to the heart. It was not taken for granted.

Momma was a deaconess in the church, and she had a deep reverence for the house of God. She did not believe in joking and playing around in God's house. She was loving, compassionate and understanding. Momma was a servant who truly enjoyed serving others. Everyone who knew her loved her also. She was charitable and full of empathy for her fellowman. Momma only attended school up to sixth grade, but you would never have perceived what little education she had when you were around her. Despite her lack of education, Momma used what she knew smartly and wisely. I saw her reading the newspaper every day after work.

Except to say that she did lots of farming and cooking with family members, Momma talked little of her childhood. She was a seamstress in her own right, and I grew up watching her at the sewing machine, zigzagging her own maternity dresses, bed spreads and curtains. I inherited my own sewing skills from Momma.

Momma kept the family together. She loved her children and shared many secrets with us. We were her little counselors. She took good care of Daddy and kept his shirts, shorts and pants immaculate. Dad's clothes were always starched and pressed, his socks and shirts white as snow. If anyone needed to know how to take care of their husband, my mother was an excellent role model and teacher.

Momma knew how to manage and save the little money that Daddy made. She was an accomplished cook who believed only in serving food that was homemade, not from a box. Momma had recipes for at least twenty different pies and cakes. I began cooking at the age of twelve, and I owe all my cooking skills to Momma, as well as to Daddy and Grandma Cora.

Grandma Cora, my mother's mother, was an awesome woman of God. She loved the Lord and loved running to His house where she sang in the choir, attended Sunday school and participated in every program held at the church. She was always there when the church doors opened.

Friends, allow me to share with you how dearly I loved my grandmother Cora. I lived with her in New York for a period of time after graduating from high school. She was my life. She was a woman of wisdom, knowledge and understanding, gifted in discerning of matters. She was also a woman that you had better not touch. If you did any harm to her, you would have been chastised by God.

Cora was a prayer warrior. Many times we prayed together before going to bed, and I frequently kneeled in prayer at her bedside early mornings and early nights. She was not one who talked the Christian life, she lived it to the fullest. She was eighty-four when she passed. For her home going service, I dressed her in my beautiful crème pearl, fish-tailed wedding dress on her final day of rest. I will always remember the wonderful things she said and did for me.

The mantle of Grandma Cora's prayer life fell to me, and my prayer life is patterned after hers. When my children were little they were taught to pray as my grandmother's teaching to me. I believe, to this day, that God imparted my grandmother's wisdom into my heart. There were so many times I wanted to walk away from the trials and tribulations of life, but Cora taught me to stand. She would guide me to "say this prayer, do this, do that." I did and I prevailed.

In closing, dear readers, I give thanks to God the Father, Son and Holy Spirit for these three wonderful people. They were the vessels of honor whom God used to mold me into the person I am today. Little did I know, growing up, that the working of the Holy Spirit was the force in their lives that made them prayer warriors. They could not have been successful without the Spirit of God leading and guiding them into all truths. Without God, they could not have had the minds to live godly lives in front of me, my brothers and sisters. The Spirit of God made them great men and women.

My friends, nothing has changed today. The same Spirit of God that motivated our predecessors into boldness, courage and strength is with us today. We cannot survive in our own strength. We need the power of the Holy Spirit to encourage us into all truths.

The word of God clearly expresses that there will be an outpouring of God's spirit, which is a prophetic promise of God. You can prepare yourself to receive the precious gift of the Holy Spirit. The Wycliffe Bible Dictionary says: *"In the NT the Holy Spirit clearly reveals Himself as a person and is Deity. He has the attributes of personality: intellect (Romans 8:27); (1 Corinthians 2:10-13), emotions (Ephesians 4:30), and will (I Corinthians 12:11). He performs the actions of personality: teaches (John 14:26), testifies (John 15:26), directs (Acts 8:29; 13:2), guides (Romans 8:14), warns (I Timothy 4:1). He is Deity because He is the Spirit of God and of Christ (Romans 8:9) and proceeds eternally from the Father."* *(John 15:26; Galatians 4:6) WBD*

The book of Psalms provides a sweet perfume description of the Holy Spirit. Psalm 133:2-3 says, *"It is like the precious ointment upon the head, that ran down upon the beard, even Aaron's beard: that went down to the skirts of his garments; As the dew of Hermon, and as the dew that descended upon the mountains of Zion: for there the Lord commanded the blessing, even life for evermore."*

So, if you attempt to live life devoid of God's inspirational force, you are pretty much doing things in your own strength and your life will be wrought with difficulty. I have made some pretty poor decisions that have resulted in unpleasant consequences and God's discipline. I recall Pastor William Prioleau in one of his TV Broadcast messages: "You don't want God to give you a whipping. The best lawyer cannot get you out of God's chastisement." This may sound comical, but it is true. Those decisions and desires that are not part of God's will for our lives will prompt much suffering and pain.

As for me, it is not a matter of choice, but rather of commitment. I desperately need the Holy Spirit directing my life. It would have been impossible for me to be where I am today, writing to you, if I were not living under the guidance of the Holy Spirit.

Letter Three

Budding
A Time for Blossoming

"The wilderness and the solitary place shall be glad for them; and the desert shall rejoice, and blossom as the rose. It shall blossom abundantly, and rejoice even with joy and singing: the glory of Lebanon shall be given unto it, the excellency of Carmel and Sharon; they shall see the glory of the Lord, and the excellency of our God." Isaiah 35:1-2

Letter Three

Budding
A Time for Blossoming

L ife's challenges often bring great disappointments. During tough times, it is easy to become overwhelmed with dark feelings of hopelessness and despair. One begins to view life as meaningless, as a bud that fails to blossom into a flower. It seems as though life is at a standstill without any hope of flourishing. A mindset of this nature has the ability to lead one into a state of deep unhappiness, which then leads to a sense of worthlessness, in believing that one's life has come to a halt. At this point, life's vision now becomes blurred as though being surrounded by smoking trees in a burning forest. With impaired vision come doubts and a lack of faith in oneself.

My question to you is, do you think it is possible for such trees to ever live again? Is there a chance of budding and blossoming again for such lifeless trees? Symbolically, as trees can come back to life, so can a life that is filled with despair be transformed into one with the conviction of hope. These periods of despair can actually become moments of opportunities wherein you can petition God for strength and the power to fight off these burdens.

Paul the Apostle encouraged the church of Philippi to rejoice and to think on the good things that will enable them to blossom. In Philippians 4:4 Paul instructs, *"Rejoice in the Lord always: and again I say Rejoice."* Then, in Philippians 4:8 he continues: *"Finally, brethren, whatsoever things are true, whatsoever things are honest, whatsoever things are just, whatsoever things are pure, whatsoever things are lovely, whatsoever things are of good report; if there be any virtue, and if there be any praise, think on these things."*

Here we find Paul encouraging the people to rejoice, to be happy and to subject their thought patterns to a new way of thinking. Friends, view your thoughts as you would upon entering into a New Year. We commit ourselves to new resolutions and so it is with our minds. Think differently. Paul returns again, this time, enforcing another change of thinking. Romans 12:2 says, *"And be not conformed to this world: but be ye transformed by the renewing of your mind, that ye may prove what is that good, and acceptable, and perfect, will of God."*

Let's take an infant as another symbol of budding and blossoming. After birth, extreme care, attention and nourishment are given to a child for its proper health and growth. As a baby is nourished, the infant grows in length, height and weight, and the child's personality begins to blossom in full. So, it is with our lives as adults.

We can re-create our own budding and blossoming, leaving behind feelings of hopelessness and despair. With God's nurturing grace, we can transform our lives with new beginnings, expanding our horizons, refreshing our goals and renewing our personal commitments, cleansing our souls, all in an effort to remove the old and to bring in the new. Think of the budding and blossoming of each spring as it comes in with fresh new scents, as flowers and trees begin to show new life. We can enjoy such a transformation in our own lives, but only with the blessings of our heavenly Father is any of this possible.

Let's hear what John has to say concerning prosperity and health. *"Beloved, I wish above all things that thou mayest prosper and be in health, even as thy soul prospereth."* (3 John: 2) As you can now understand, God is concerned about our physical and spiritual well being, which is part of the blossoming process.

We need the guidance of God through this flowering process. When we are obedient to the will and call of God in our lives, we become blessed people. Not only are we blessed but our children are granted blessings, as is stated in Psalm 115:14. *"The Lord shall increase you more and more, you and your children."*

God gave Joshua specific instructions in what to do in order to prosper. These are the promises and instructions God gave to him as we read in Joshua 1:4: *"From the wilderness and this Lebanon even unto the great river, the river Euphrates, all the land of the Hittites, and unto the Great Sea toward the going down of the sun, shall be your coast."* God continues in Joshua 1:8, *"This book of the law shall not depart out of thy mouth; but thou shalt meditate therein day and night, that thou mayest observe to do according to all that is written therein: for then thou shalt make thy way prosperous, and then thou shalt have good success."* This was the commandment God gave to Joshua. Had he failed to follow God's directives, he would not have blossomed in "good success."

When we obey the call of God, our lives will bud and blossom like flowers on a tree. You may be succeeding in your own strength, but in the end you will need the new growth of God's love to prosper. So, my dear readers, may I leave you with a question? Is your life budding and blossoming into a new life in God?

Letter Four

The Pecan Dream

"Then saith he unto his disciples, The harvest truly is plenteous, but the laborers are few; Pray ye therefore the Lord of the harvest, that he will send forth laborers into his harvest." Matthew 9:37-38

Letter Four

The Pecan Dream

I n this dream a very large box arrived at my home. I opened it to discover a bounty of beautiful, fully-ripened pecans. These pecans were obviously the result of a farmer's labor as he cultivated and nourished his trees in the production of such a generous harvest.

The next day in quiet meditation, I pondered within my heart as to the interpretation of my dream. I asked the Lord to reveal the meaning. Here is what the Lord spoke into my spirit: at the hand of the Lord an abundance of great blessings shall fall upon me. These blessings shall flow as the blessings of the widow of Zarephath. 1 Kings 17:14 says, *"For thus saith the LORD God of Israel, the barrel of meal shall not waste, neither shall the cruse of oil fail, until the day that the Lord sendeth rain upon the earth."*

I was then taken to the book of Joshua, Joshua 1:8, which states: *"But thou shalt meditate therein day and night, that thou mayest observe to do according to all that is written therein: for then thou shalt make thy way prosperous, and then thou shalt have good success."* Reading this passage from Joshua confirmed to me the message of the Pecan Dream, that we must work in order to be successful. As the farmer planted, so would I. One must have faith that he will be successful in what has been divinely revealed. So, my friends, I have lots of work to do. James says, *"Even so faith, if it hath not works, is dead, being alone. Yea, a man say, Thou hast faith, and I have works: show me thy faith without thy works, and I will show thee my faith by my works."* (James 2:17-18)

Let's take a journey back to the widow woman of Zarephath and all that she had done to receive her blessing. She planted a seed (blessing) into the life of the man of God, Elijah, the Prophet. The seed: "And *Elijah said unto her, Fear not; go and do as thou hast said: but make me thereof a little cake first, and bring it unto me, and after make for thee and for thy son."* (I Kings 17:13)

Elijah was on his last leg. God gave Elijah direct orders to travel to the city of Zarephath to the widow woman and her son. The widow woman believed Elijah and gave him her last meal. See I Kings 17:9-12. Being a woman of faith and good works, the widow gave no thought to her physical hunger, only to the hunger for God. Because of her obedience and sacrifice, she and her son did not lack for food. I Kings 17:15 says: *"And she went and did according to the saying of Elijah: and she, and he, and her house, did eat many days."* Jesus says: *"He that receiveth a prophet in the name of a prophet shall receive a prophet's reward."* (Matthew 10:41a)

The farmer who produced the pecans in my dream had to have a vision to grow a crop of such beauty. This is what the book of Proverbs says, *"Where there is no vision, the people perish."* (Proverbs 29:18a) When we are given a vision, let's not forget to include the cost. In Luke, Jesus says: *"For which of you, intending to build a tower, sitteth not down first, and counteth the cost, whether he have sufficient to finish it?"* (Luke 14:28)

Can we say that the farmer accomplished the goal of his vision? Before purchasing, he surveyed the land to determine if he was investing in fertile ground for the planting of the crop. As is stated in Joshua 2:1, *"And Joshua the son of Nun sent out of Shittim two men to spy secretly, saying, Go view the land, even Jericho."* The farmer then dug the irrigation trenches, planted the seeds and applied fertilizer for many years to yield a harvest of such magnitude. And he must have experienced many sleepless nights worrying about his crop. Thus, the "cost."

In the book of Nehemiah, he is found with a personal vision to rebuild the walls of Jerusalem. He inspected the walls prior to rebuilding. Scripture tells us that Nehemiah was a private man—he worked quietly. The Bible says in Nehemiah 2:15, *"Then went I up in the night by the brook, and viewed the wall, and turned back, and entered by the gate of the valley, and so returned."* One must have a mind to work. Says Nehemiah: *"for the people had a mind to work."* (Nehemiah 4:6)

There is much laboring in Christian farming, but the effort produces a great harvest of souls. The Bible encourages work: *"There is nothing better for a man, than that he should eat and drink, and that he should make his soul enjoy good in his labor. This also I saw, that it was from the hand of God."* (Ecclesiastes 2:24)

The illustration of Christian farming is to enlighten your hearts to the many souls that are yet to come into the kingdom of God. Few are willing to labor in the vineyard of the Lord, as the pecan farmer. Jesus tells us in Luke 10:2a, *"The harvest truly is great, but the laborers are few."* Christian farmers are soul planters. Paul reminds the church of Corinth, *"I have planted, Apollos watered; but God gave the increase."*(1 Corinthians 3:6) In other words, we minister to the soul—God pierces the heart.

I encourage you to focus attention on the farmer, the widow woman, Elijah the prophet, Nehemiah and the laborer. The widow's obedience brought her a blessed harvest; the farmer, beautiful pecans. A harvest comes only after a seed has been sown. When one plants apple seeds, a harvest of apples is expected. So, it is with our lives today. We are encouraged to become planters and visionaries.

As you read this letter today, consider the benefits of farming. Deposit good seeds into your bodies, finances and into your lives. Who knows what your tomorrow may bring. Perhaps it will produce a beautiful Pecan Dream as I have shared. I believe in dreams. I've had many dreams that have come to pass. I trust that you have enjoyed my dream.

Letter Five

Fugitive Jonah

"And I said, Oh that I had wings like a dove! for then would I fly away, and be at rest."
Psalm 55:6

Letter Five

Fugitive Jonah

*F*ugitive Jonah is dedicated to all those on the run from the Lord Jesus Christ. Jonah, God is calling you. He has been knocking at your door, your heart, for a long time. Why are you still running? Don't you admit that it's time to cross over into Jordan, a place of blessings given freely by God?

Jonah ran from the Lord. The Bible says: *"Now the word of the Lord came unto Jonah the son of Amittai, saying, Arise, go to Nineveh, that great city, and cry against it; for their wickedness is come up before me. But Jonah rose up to flee unto Tarshish from the presence of the Lord, and went down to Joppa; and he found a ship going to Tarshish: so he paid the fare thereof, and went down into it, to go with them unto Tarshish from the presence of the Lord."* (Jonah 1:1-3) God is everywhere at the same time and place. He is all powerful and all knowing. It is impossible for you to run from the presence of God. He knows everything there is to know about you. Make no mistake, the Bible makes it clear: God is all-knowing. Scripture tells us, *"O Lord, thou has searched me, and known me. Thou knowest my downsitting and mine uprising; thou understandest my thought afar off."*

(Psalm 139:1-2) *"If I ascend up into heaven, thou art there: if I make my bed in hell, behold, thou art there."* (Psalm 139:8)

Allow me to share my Jonah experience. Before surrendering my life to Christ, I was a Fugitive Jonah on the run from God. In the early 1980s before I met my second husband, I was living in New York City. It was there that I encountered all kinds of people. I got caught up with the wrong crowd and was in bad relationships. I went to places I had no business going to. One weekend, a friend and I drove from New York to South Carolina to visit another friend, where we ended up spending the weekend. From there, we went to another house where drugs were being sold. As we entered, we were shrouded in smoke so thick that it was as though we were in a white forest. Throughout the house, people were getting high and free-basing. I became upset and afraid and told my friend that I wanted to leave.

My friend and I walked out of that scene, but there were other times that I ended up in the wrong place, even hanging out in basements of night clubs, watching addicts snorting cocaine and smoking marijuana. Several of them died from drug overdoses. Others were shot and killed in drug fights in the street. Thankfully, although I was not fully committed to God at that time, He kept me strong enough not to turn to a life of drugs.

But I continued with my dangerous ways. I would go out to the clubs during the week and parties on Friday and Saturday nights. Eventually, my reckless living almost cost me my life. I was involved with a man who had another girlfriend, and she decided to blow my head off, literally! She went to my place of work with the intention of shooting me as I came off the elevator. It was only her confusion about which elevator I was using that saved my life. The devil's plot that day was to kill me as I walked off that elevator— but, God's plan outwitted the devil. The Bible records: *"For my thoughts are not your thoughts, neither are your ways my ways, saith the Lord. For as the heavens are higher than the earth, so are my ways higher than your ways, and my thoughts than your thoughts."* (Isaiah 55:8-9) The devil thought he had me, but God showed Satan that He was in control of my life.

Despite the fact that I was not living according to the standards of God, I loved the church, my spiritual foundation. I knew that, on Sunday, church was where I belonged. When I arrived, the Spirit of God conquered me; my heavy heart was lifted up. I felt empty and dry as a dried-out prune, but I often entered the house of God and found myself in Pastor Joe L. Brown's office requesting prayer. I feared sharing what I had done the night before. My heart was sick and stunk from Saturday night's sins. And after the pastor prayed and my spirit was lifted, I felt better until the following week when I was back again repeating my sins. Each time after committing those sinful acts against God, the spirit of death came upon me. I cried for days, begging and pleading with God to forgive my trespasses.

God knew that I had a sincere heart. He knew it was my desire to live a clean holy life but that I did not have the strength of the Holy Spirit's power to pull myself out of guilt and shame. God does not judge us on the surface. He judges our inner heart. Scripture says, *"I the Lord search the heart, I try the reins, even to give every man according to his ways, and according to the fruit of his doing."* (Jeremiah 17:10) God protected me from the hand of the enemy for this very hour, day and purpose—that my life would be a living testimony for you. God can deliver you when you are at your lowest. He will pick you up and hold you in the palm of His hand.

On Saturday, October 19, 1985, I was no longer a Fugitive Jonah. God changed my entire life. He saved my soul from a burning hell. Yes, that is exactly where I was headed if God had not stepped in with a rescue plan. I can still recall vividly what transpired that morning when an earthquake shook the city. I was asleep when suddenly the entire apartment building was vibrating. The bed moved as though I was on a ship being tossed by high waves. The venetian blinds and dishes in the kitchen cabinets were rattling loudly, and pictures were falling off the walls.

I immediately jumped out of bed with the terrified feeling that the world was coming to an end. I said "Oh, my God, God is coming back and I am not saved." I ran to my children, pulled them out of bed and cried, "We must pray. God is coming back." Friends, from that very moment, I stopped running from the voice of God. He saved me that morning, and I became a true Christian because I stopped lying to myself, I admitted that the life I was living was destroying my soul.

That day, I surrendered my life to Christ. I was a changed person, and those who knew me saw the change. That morning I called friends who I knew would be going to church, and I asked to be picked up for Saturday service. From that point on, I found myself in church on Saturday and Sunday nights rather than in night clubs and other places of sin and destruction. I knew that I was finally home.

Fugitive Jonah, God is calling you. God said in Isaiah 65:1-3, *"I am sought of them that asked not for me; I am found of them that sought me not: I said, Behold me, behold me, unto a nation that was not called by my name. I have spread out my hands all the day unto a rebellious people, which walketh in a way that was not good, after their own thoughts; A people that provoketh me to anger continually to my face."*

This is a CALL OUT to all of you Fugitive Jonahs to surrender to God. God is not your enemy. He is your friend. Scripture states: *"A man that hath friends must show him-*

self friendly: and there is a friend that sticketh closer than a brother." (Proverbs 18:24)

As I end this Letter, please consider these questions:

Are you a Fugitive Jonah on the run?

Was that you driving home drunk Saturday night? Did your car flip over several times, landing in a ditch in FRONT OF THE CHURCH? Was that you who walked away from that accident with no broken bones?

Are you the one that the police officer did not question or examine to see if you were drunk? Was the grace of God upon you that night because you did not get arrested?

Was the favor of God upon you the time that you were arrested in your mess, when you stayed in jail overnight but walked out the next day? Would you not say that it was the grace of God that brought you out?

Are you still cursing out your mother, father, pastor, friend or family member who loves you dearly and continues to invite you to church or prayer meeting? Are you still responding, "Tell me nothing about church. I don't want to hear that sermon. I am not coming to church. I will come when I am ready and not when you say so. This is my life, and I am going to live it the way I want until the day I die." Do these words sound familiar to you?

Are you still drinking, partying and hanging with the wrong crowd who have nothing to offer you? Has a bullet missed you just as the one that barely missed me?

Do you think it is because of your own ingenuity that you are still breathing life?

My dear friends, kid not yourselves. Sin will be judged. The Bible records in Psalm 96:13, *"Before the Lord: for he cometh to judge the earth: he shall judge the world with righteousness, and the people with his truth."* Then, as Hebrews 9:27 warns us, *"And it is appointed unto men once to die, but after this the judgment."*

Letter Six

The Painful Cost of Disobedience

"Behold, to obey is better than sacrifice, and to hearken than the fat of rams." I Samuel 15:22

Letter Six

The Painful Cost of Disobedience

A re you rebellious and disobedient to God? If you answered yes to this question, fear not, delivery is on the way. You can receive deliverance in the midst of reading, this very moment. God is so merciful, loving and kind. But never take God's goodness for granted. Even though He is a forgiving God, He can be a God of wrath. You want to avoid the judgment of God.

In the book of Jeremiah, Chapter 3, the tribe of Judah turns from the Lord to become a disobedient and rebellious people. God commissioned Jeremiah: *"Go and proclaim these words toward the north, and say, Return, thou backsliding Israel, saith the Lord; and I will not cause mine anger to fall upon you: for I am merciful, saith the Lord, and I will not keep anger for ever."* (Jeremiah 3:12) If you read closely, that was an appeal from God: people of Judah, return to the Lord your God. Again, God makes another plea in Jeremiah 3:14-15, *"Turn, O backsliding children, saith the LORD; for I am married unto you: and I will take you one of a city, and two of a family, and I will bring you to Zion: And I will give you pastors according to mine heart, which shall feed you with knowledge and understanding."* God not only makes an appeal to return, but He stands ready to forgive sin and to bless the tribe with pastors who will feed (teach) the word of truth, the word of God, with knowledge and understanding.

Throughout the book of Jeremiah, we read that God consistently implores Judah in Jeremiah 7:3: *"Amend your ways and your doings, and I will cause you to dwell in this place."* But as the people of the tribe continue in sin, the wrath of God builds. He instructs Jeremiah as we read in Jeremiah 7:16, *"Therefore pray not thou for this people, neither lift up cry nor prayer for them, neither make intercession to me: for I will not hear thee."*

My dear readers, remember that all you do in life must be pleasing in the sight of God. Not your ways but God's ways. Isaiah 55:7 says, *"Let the wicked forsake his way, and the unrighteous man his thoughts: and let him return unto the LORD, and he will have mercy upon him; and to our God, for he will abundantly pardon."* So, believe not for one moment finite minds can outsmart an infinitely wise and powerful God.

God's message to you is to let go of your unrighteous thoughts and ways. They will lead you down a dead end street. Wouldn't it be wise to follow God's roadmap, the Holy Bible? God will always be there for you. He is calling and reaching out to you this very moment. Let's read what God says in Isaiah 55:1. *"Ho, every one that thirsteth, come ye to the waters, and he that hath no money; come ye, buy, and eat; yea, come, buy wine and milk without money and without price."*

Readers, this is a plea from a very loving God. Meditate on these words and see what God is saying to your heart. He is there for you with out-stretched arms as He was to a rebellious nation that was not thinking of him. God's desire is to be Lord and Savior over your life, but He is not going to force Himself upon you. God has made His creatures free agents. You have the opportunity to choose who you will serve in life.

Joshua said to the tribes of Israel: *"And if it seem evil unto you to serve the LORD, choose you this day whom ye will serve; whether the gods which your fathers served that were on the other side of the flood, or the gods of the Amorites, in whose land ye dwell: but as for me and my house, we will serve the Lord."* (Joshua 24:15) Joshua made it known to Israel whose side he was on, and he gave the people an ultimatum—God or idol gods?

Disobedience will be judged. God will not allow sin to continue forever. Romans 6:1-2 confirms judgment: *"What shall we say then? Shall we continue in sin, that grace may abound? God forbid. How shall we, that are dead to sin, live any longer therein?"* Make the commitment to yourself: today is my last day of being disobedient. I am not going to commit this willful act against God anymore. According to Romans 6:1-2, sin *"has its season."*

If you are one whom God has delivered from a life of sin and rebellion, don't look back to that life again. There are consequences to looking back. Those who look back shall suffer loss. In Genesis Chapter 19, God told Lot to leave Sodom. God was going to destroy Sodom because of sin. Lot's wife looked back: *"But his wife looked back from behind him, and she became a pillar of salt."* (Genesis 19:26) So, my dear readers, this is a biblical warning not to look back once God has delivered you.

Pray to God for strength to endure your weakest and darkest hours. God can deliver you in the midst of reading this letter. There's nothing too hard for God. Jeremiah 32:27 says, *"Behold, I am the LORD, the God of all flesh: is there any thing too hard for me?"* Dear readers, God has presented you with a very serious question—think on it.

God is waiting on you to surrender to him. He calls you to repentance, and He makes a special appeal to you in Isaiah

113

1:18-19: *"Come now, and let us reason together, saith the LORD: though your sins be as scarlet, they shall be as white as snow; though they be red like crimson, they shall be as wool."*

One day, you too will say as I have: *"I WAITED patiently for the LORD; and he inclined unto me, and heard my cry. He brought me up also out of a horrible pit, out of the miry clay, and set my feet upon a rock, and established my goings."* (Psalm 40:1-2)

Don't look back—stay in the "PRESS". Philippians 3:13-14 says, *"Brethern, I count not myself to have apprehended: but this one thing I do, forgetting those things which are behind, and reaching forth unto those things which are before. I press toward the mark for the prize of the high calling of God in Christ Jesus."*

This very hour, I pray you will answer the high calling of God to His way, will and purpose for your life. He awaits you with open arms and, if you respond, your life will never be the same again.

Letter Seven

Pray In Faith and Confidence

"And this is the confidence that we have in him, that, if we ask any thing according to his will, he heareth us." I John 5:14

Letter Seven

Pray in Faith and Confidence

I've learned much about what prayer really is. I give credit for my prayer life to the late Mother Mildred Scott, along with my grandmother Cora. They made me a powerful prayer warrior.

I recall a Sunday morning, early upon entering the sanctuary. Mother walked up to me and told me that she wanted me to start off the prayer that morning. I was stunned by her request and gave the excuse that I was assigned as an usher for that morning's service. Mother simply replied, "You have to pray before you can usher." Today I can look back and laugh at this episode, but at the time, I could not laugh. Why? I was not yet truly molded nor grounded in serious prayer. Nonetheless, since that day, I am always ready, willing and available to kick off prayer, anytime or anywhere, in full boldness of the Lord.

Mother also said, "When you first begin to pray, it may seem as though you are not feeling anything, but just keep praying and the anointing will come." When you begin to pray but are lost for words with no idea about what to say, just open your mouth and the Spirit of God will speak for you. The Bible says, "*Likewise the Spirit also helpeth our infirmities: for we know not what we should pray for as we ought: but the Spirit itself maketh intercession for us with groanings which cannot be uttered. And he that searcheth the hearts knoweth what is the mind of the Spirit, because he maketh intercession for the saints according to the will of God."* (Romans 8:26-27)

Today, I am a witness that prayer works. The more you pray, the more powerful you become. You will begin to see supernatural miracles and the healing of the sick right before your eyes. You will begin to take joy in seeing others surrender their lives to Christ through powerful prayer. You will see the restoration of marriages, observe unemployed people finding jobs and significant changes in your place of business. Your prayer can change your neighborhood. Your prayer life can change your children. Prayer can change a person's heart from evil to good, and that person will never be able to comprehend why he experienced his change of heart. But you will know—you prayed the word of God. The Bible says, *"The king's heart is in the hand of the Lord, as the rivers of water: he turneth it whithersoever he will."* (Proverbs 21:1) Pastor William Prioleau teaches us to pray in the scripture. Even greater things happen when you learn how to pray in scriptures.

The Bible constantly reminds us: *"Pray without ceasing."* (1 Thessalonians 5:17) When you suffer under a heavy burden, remember the words of the Bible, *"Casting all your care upon him; for he careth for you."* (1 Peter 5:7) When you feel the pressures of the world overtaking you, pray Psalm 61:2: *"From the end of the earth will I cry unto thee, when my heart is overwhelmed. Lead me to the rock that is higher than I."* When you are expecting an answer from God, consider Psalm 62:5: *"My soul, wait thou only upon God; for my expectation is from him."*

Elijah was a praying man. First, he prayed to God that it might not rain; then he went back to God and prayed for rain.

The Bible says, *"Elijah was a man subject to like passions as we are, and he prayed earnestly that it might not rain: and it rained not on the earth by the space of three years and six months. And he prayed again, and the heaven gave rain, and the earth brought forth her fruit."* (James 5:17-18)

God is a prayer answering God. What His word promises will be delivered. The Bible says in Isaiah 55:11, *"So shall my word be that goeth forth out of my mouth: it shall not return unto me void, but it shall accomplish that which I please, and it shall prosper in the thing whereto I sent it."* Then, Numbers 23:19 says, *"God is not a man, that he should lie; neither the son of man, that he should repent: hath he said, and shall he not do it? Or hath he spoken, and shall he not make it good?"*

God wants us to call upon Him in trouble. There's nothing that we are facing today that is too hard for Him to handle. Jeremiah 32:27 says, *"Behold, I am the LORD, the God of all flesh: is there anything too hard for me?"* Then, Jeremiah 33:3 says, *"Call unto me, and I will answer thee, and show thee great and mighty things, which thou knowest not."*

My friends, in closing, it is vital that when you pray, do so in faith and confidence. Believe that what you have prayed for has already been granted. You are simply waiting in patience on its manifestation. 1 John 5:14-15 says pray in confidence: *"And this is the confidence that we have in him, that, if we ask any thing according to his will, he heareth us: And if we know that he hear us, whatsoever we ask, we know that we have the petitions that we desired of him."* Believing in the manifestation requires faith. Hebrews 11:1 says, *"Now faith is the substance of things hoped for, the evidence of things not seen."*

This letter, Pray in Faith and Confidence, is written in memory of Mother Mildred Scott. She was a wonderful woman of God. She loved the Lord and left behind a legacy of love and prayers. She was certainly a praying woman. If you stayed around her long enough, her prayer mantle would rest upon you too. Mother was a woman of purpose and a visionary. She pursued life with a purpose. If Mother saw purpose in you, she pursued. Many became prayer warriors under her leadership. She believed and trusted in me, frequently reminding me, *"I can depend on you. You are my backup person."* These words gave me hope and encouragement. Mother is greatly missed at the Evening of Prayer.

Deacon Scott, you too are a prayer warrior. I enjoyed your prayerful testimony on many occasions as you described the effects of your wife's prayers upon your life. Thank you, Deacon Scott and family, for sharing your lovely wife and mother with us.

Letter Eight

Symptoms of a Spiritual Stroke

"But he was wounded for our transgressions, he was bruised for our iniquities: the chastisement of our peace was upon him; and with his stripes we are healed." Isaiah 53:5

Letter Eight

Symptoms of a Spiritual Stroke

F riends, please allow me to take you back and reflect on my life. As you have read in *Letters of Encouragement*, I have undergone many spiritual surgeries. Many times I was in and out of hospitals, suffering from sins and experiencing spiritual strokes that made me feel worthless. I knew my life was out of order but could not repair the damage myself. I was incapable of performing spiritual open heart surgery on myself. I did not have the tools. It was only after suffering stroke after stoke in my soul and admitting myself into the Spiritual Hospital that I was born again and saved by the blood of Jesus.

In the natural realm, a stroke can be very devastating, leaving one paralyzed and immobile with the loss of ability to function. Many have had strokes without any warnings or signs. Some had warnings yet ignored them. After a stroke, impairment leaves one with little sign of hope and feeling that life has ended. Therapy treatment afterward is recommended to regain strength.

In the spiritual realm, you can find yourself in the same state of mind. Yet, in both cases, there is help. At the first sign of a spiritual stroke you can call on JESUS—verbally. Yes—J-E-S-U-S is your emergency doctor.

Let's take a close look at the symptoms of a Spiritual Stroke: You first begin to experience a numbness or weakness in the Word of God. Your spiritual mind has become weary; you are now in need of a spiritual pinch—a word of encouragement. Your countenance has changed. Bright glory no longer shines on your face. Revelation 3:16 says, *"Thou art lukewarm, and neither cold nor hot."* You have become bitter-sweet in God. You are spiritually limp in your arms and legs. You've lost your strength, and you no longer feel the desire to dance like David.

This behavior is not acceptable to God. Revelation 3:15-16 says, *"I know thy works, that thou art neither cold nor hot: I would thou wert cold or hot. So then because thou art lukewarm, and neither cold nor hot, I will spew thee out of my mouth."* Wow, let's take a tip from David. If anyone was hot for God and knew how to praise, it was David. David loved the Lord heartily: *"the Lord hath sought him a man after his own heart."* (I Samuel 13:14b)

2 Samuel 6:14-15 says, *"And David danced before the Lord with all his might; and David was girded with a linen ephod. So David and all the house of Israel brought up the ark of the Lord with shouting, and with the sound of the trumpet."*

Now that you realize that you have suffered a spiritual stroke, it's time to check into a Spiritual Hospital—damages to be assessed. You are about to undergo a series of tests to discover if these are symptoms of a spiritual stroke. If this is you, you can rest assured that the deliverer Jesus can and will deliver you.

Spiritual Memory Loss

You are unable to think properly, have a loss of memory and now have a different frame of mind. The results for this test indicate failure. You have trouble remembering the words of Isaiah and Philippians: *"Thou wilt keep him in perfect peace, whose mind is stayed on thee: because he trusteth in thee."* (Isaiah 26:3) *"Let this mind be in you, which was also in Christ Jesus."* (Philippians 2:5)

In other words, you have lost your peace and you no longer have the mind of Christ. You failed to heed the words of Paul. Romans 12:1-2 says, *"I Beseech you therefore, brethren, by the mercies of God, that ye present your bodies a living sacrifice, holy, acceptable unto God, which is your reasonable service. And be not conformed to this world: but be ye transformed by the renewing of your mind, that ye may prove what is that good, and acceptable, and perfect, will of God."*

Your memory has become like withered grass. Isaiah 40:7 declares, *"the grass withereth, the flower fadeth."* Spiritual Memory Loss is the end result of not spending quality time with God, failing to study the word of God and failure to saturate your mind in good spiritual books. God can restore your memory. He promised to keep your mind in perfect peace.

Spiritual Blood Pressure

Your blood pressure is very low. You're now experiencing feelings of fatigue and tiredness. At this point you really feel like throwing in the towel. You are now at the point where you have no energy. Discouragement has set in and now you are exhausted. Due to the fact that you've not been spending quality time with God, your blood pressure test shows that you have a deficiency in your red blood cells (which represents the blood of Jesus). Your pressure can be revived by repentance—asking God for forgiveness for laziness, not reading the word and not spending time with God. Your spiritual pressure will immediately elevate.

God strengthens in time of weakness. Isaiah 40:29 tells us, *"He giveth power to the faint; and to them that have no might he increaseth strength."*

In your lowest moments, God will strengthen you like an eagle. Isaiah 40:31 says, *"But they that wait upon the Lord shall renew their strength; they shall mount up with wings as eagles; they shall run, and not be weary; and they shall walk, and not faint."*

Spiritual Dizziness

At this point you are really out of balance. You have become confused, running from one place to the other trying to discover reasons for your dizziness. You have forgotten what the bible says about running here and there. Ephesians 4:14 informs us, *"That we henceforth be no more children, tossed to and fro, and carried about with every wind of doctrine, by the sleight of men and cunning craftiness, whereby they lie in wait to deceive."*

You're suffering from a lack of spiritual stability. You don't have the boldness to stand for God as you once did. At this point you have been diagnosed with a rare blood deficiency—spiritual dizziness. An injection of the Holy Spirit will revive you back to life. Allow me to share with you a few proven scriptures that will open your eyes to this fact: Ephesians 5:18-19 says, *"And be not drunk with wine, wherein is excess; but be filled with the Spirit; Speaking to yourselves in psalms and hymns and spiritual songs, singing and making melody in your heart to the Lord."*

God can put you back in balance, rotate your spiritual tires and get you back on track with a bountiful, fruitful prayer and fasting life.

Friends, today, allow God to give you a booster shot of his power and glory. He will fill your spiritual gas tank with scriptures. Being filled with the word of God prevents spiritual dizziness.

In closing, remember, God is reaching out to you. He wants to abort these signs and symptoms of spiritual stroke before they can reach your spiritual vital organs. He's reaching out to you, He's calling you. In Isaiah 65:1-2, He tells us, *"I am sought of them that asked not for me; I am found of them that sought me not: I said, Behold me, behold me, unto a nation that was not called by my name. I have spread out my hands all the day unto a rebellious people, which walketh in a way that was not good, after their own thoughts."*

Accept the call today of our Lord and Savior Jesus Christ. He loves and cares for you. No one can love you as Jesus does.

Letter Nine

Petition Granted

"Call unto me, and I will answer thee, and show thee great and mighty things, which thou knowest not." Jeremiah 33:3

Letter Nine

Petition Granted

It is significantly imperative that we abide in the will of God. Many of us are living outside of His will in a fast moving society. We desire to have it our way: easy, quick and fast. We can have it—easy, quick and fast—if we do it God's way. The Bible says in Psalm 37:4-5, *"Delight thyself also in the Lord; and he shall give thee the desires of thine heart. Commit thy way unto the LORD; trust also in him; and he shall bring it to pass."* The Bible states that God will give us our desires, Psalm 84:11c: *"No good thing will he withhold from them that walk uprightly."* In other words, you must meet the conditions of God: live uprightly, live righteously, honorably and morally in the presence of God.

Let's take a look at what the Bible says about Jabez in 1 Chronicles 4:9-10. *"And Jabez was more honorable than his brethren: and his mother called his name Jabez, saying, Because I bare him with sorrow. And Jabez called on the God of Israel, saying, Oh that thou wouldest bless me indeed, and enlarge my coast, and that thine hand might be with me, and that thou wouldest keep me from evil, that it may not grieve me! And God granted him that which he requested."*

What an awesome petition! God gave Jabez the desires of his heart because he was "more honorable than his brethren." It was God's will: *"Beloved, I wish above all things that thou mayest prosper and be in health, even as thy soul prospereth."* (3 John: 2) As the Scripture says, Jabez's request was in order: *"Let all things be done decently and in order."* (1 Corinthians 14:40) Jabez did not ask amiss. James 4:3 says, *"Ye ask, and receive not, because ye ask amiss, that ye may consume it upon your lusts."* So, my friends, can we say that Jabez was careful in his request to God?

Go with me to the book of Acts where we find Paul and Silas in the midst of a crisis. They were thrown into jail for baptizing, healing and preaching the gospel of Jesus Christ. (Acts 16:23) But at midnight, as they prayed, God came to their rescue, as we see in Acts 16:26, *"And suddenly there was a great earthquake, so that the foundations of the prison were shaken: and immediately all the doors were opened, and every one's bands were loosed."* God granted their petition and performed a miracle, delivering Paul and Silas from jail. So, let's read on to discover another miracle, the one that God performed in granting Hannah her petition.

Hannah, a wonderful woman of God, was in the midst of her own midnight crisis. She was married to Elkanah who had two wives at the same time. According to 1 Samuel 1:2, *"And he had two wives; the name of the one was Hannah, and the name of the other Peninnah: and Peninnah had children, but Hannah had not children."* And then, 1 Samuel 1:5a says, *"But the Lord had shut up her womb."* Friends, follow me, allow me to take you on a spiritual midnight ride.

A midnight crisis does not necessarily mean it's midnight. A midnight crisis can occur when a loved one walks out on you, when you've lost a loved one in death, you've failed a test, lost your job or your home. It can be any situation that the enemy has placed upon you.

Hannah wept and grieved because she bore no children unto her husband. The Scripture says, *"Then said Elkanah her husband to her, Hannah, why weepest thou? and why eatest thou not? and why is thy heart grieved? am not I better to thee than ten sons?"* (1 Samuel 1:8) Sometimes, it is difficult for others to understand our deepest pain. Hannah knew that there was only one answer out of her barrenness— prayer! The Bible says in 1 Samuel 1:10-11 that she went to the temple and made a vow to God: *"And she was in bitterness of soul, and prayed unto the Lord, and wept sore. And she vowed a vow, and said, O LORD of hosts, if thou wilt indeed look on the affliction of thine handmaid, and remember me, and not forget thine handmaid, but wilt give unto thine handmaid a man child, then I will give him unto the LORD all the days of his life, and there shall no razor come upon his head."*

Then, the Bible states: *"So the woman went her way, and did eat, and her countenance was no more sad."* (1 Samuel 1:18) We can now say that Hannah prayed in faith believing God that a shifting had taken place and that she was coming out of her midnight crisis. God heard and gave Hannah the desire of her heart. Note: Hannah asked in "specifics"— she asked for a man child. Remember, when presenting your request before God it should always be according to God's will and not for personal gain. You want God to get the glory.

God got the glory, and Scripture says Hannah gave birth to a man child named Samuel. Scripture informs us in 1 Samuel 1:20 as follows: *"Wherefore it came to pass, when the time was come about after Hannah had conceived, that she bare a son, and called his name Samuel, saying, Because I have asked him of the LORD."*

Hannah kept the vow she had committed unto the Lord. 1 Samuel 1:24-28 says, *"And when she had weaned him, she took him up with her, with three bullocks, and one ephah of flour, and a bottle of wine, and brought him unto the house of the LORD in Shiloh: and the child was young. And they slew a bullock, and brought the child to Eli. And she said, Oh my Lord, as thy soul liveth, my lord, I am the woman that stood by thee here, praying unto the LORD. For this child I prayed; and the LORD hath given me my petition which I asked of him: Therefore also I have lent him to the LORD; as long as he liveth he shall be lent to the LORD. And he worshipped the LORD there."*

Goodness, what a beautiful miracle! God can do the same for you today. What He did for Hannah, He will do for you today. Only trust and believe.

In closing, allow me to share the story of my own barrenness. In 1974, I experienced great difficulty conceiving and underwent multiple tests, but nothing worked. The doctor finally informed me that he had done all he knew how to do. His last words to me were, "I'm so sorry my dear, but the best thing for you is adoption. The only way you can have a child is with the help of God." Well, little did the doctor know that his words were inspiring words that increased my faith in God's assistance. I left his office, went straight home and prayed this prayer: "God, if it is your will, please give me a child. Lord, if you give me a child, I promise I will give him back to you in life." Two months later I conceived. Praise God! He blessed my husband and me with a healthy baby boy. Today he is 37.

I did not retract my promise. From my son's infancy through his graduation from high school, I gave Isaiah back to the Lord. We ran to the house of God on every available opportunity. The Bible says, *"Train up a child in the way he should go: and when he is old, he will not depart from it."* (Proverbs 22:6) I kept my vow and the commitment that I had made to the Lord. The Bible says, *"When thou vowest a vow unto God, defer not to pay it; for he hath no pleasure in fools: pay that which thou hast vowed. Better is it that thou shouldest not vow, than that thou shouldest vow and not pay.*

Suffer not thy mouth to cause thy flesh to sin; neither say thou before the angel, that it was an error: wherefore should God be angry at thy voice, and destroy the work of thine hands?" (Ecclesiastes 5:4-6)

Just as He answered the petitions of Hannah and Jabez and He fulfilled my request for a child, God will visit you too in your barrenness. He can do any and every thing—except fail. There is no failure in God. Friends, I pray that you have been blessed in reading about the greatness of God! Do not underestimate His power and mercy. God stands ready to grant you your petition.

Letter Ten

Real Love Comes from the Heart

"And though I bestow all my goods to feed the poor, and though I give my body to be burned, and have not charity, it profiteth me nothing." I Corinthians 13:3

Letter Ten

Real Love Comes from the Heart

L ove is an action word. It speaks, can reveal signs and hide many faults. I Peter 4:8 says, *"And above all things have fervent charity among yourselves: for charity shall cover the multitude of sins."* Love explodes when it speaks. It is one of the most powerful spoken words of today. Love is powerful and, if you're not careful, it can turn your life upside down. Love, the wrong kind of love, will place you in a position of doing things that you normally would not do. Love has made many commit heinous crimes. Love can turn into jealousy and hate if you're not careful. Love will make you do things you know are wrong. Love has the capability of placing one in destructive relationships. True love is embedded deep in the heart.

Friends, can I be real with you? May I speak the truth? In my introduction to *Letters of Encouragement*, I stated that everything I have written is truth. Friends, the wrong kind of love made me do some awful things when I was out of the will of God. I did things that hurt others, as I am sure that you too have hurt others. We all have a past life that God has delivered us from. Thank God for His grace and mercy.

I communicated with you initially that I grew up in church and was raised by godly parents. My parents taught me well. Many times my mother as well as my grandmother instructed me to stay away from a so called love relationship. I did not listen. I was madly and blindly in love. Friends, let's take a tip from each other's experiences. Know surely that if you play around in a bad relationship, trouble lies ahead. The bible cautions in Proverbs 6:27, *"Can a man take fire in his bosom, and his clothes not be burned?"* Then, Proverbs 6:28 says, *"Can one go upon hot coals, and his feet not be burned?"*

Burned, of course, represents trouble. If you're in a relationship and you're the one who is always giving and consistently suffering hurt and pain—take heed—run before the fire gets too hot. 2 Corinthians 6:14 cautions*: "Be ye not unequally yoked together with unbelievers: for what fellowship hath righteousness with unrighteousness? And what communion hath light with darkness?"*

If you love the Lord and your desire is to have a mate, wait on God. He will deliver. Seek God. Matthew 6:33 states: *"But seek ye first the kingdom of God, and his righteousness; and all these things shall be added unto you."* You must first get busy with the things of God. Another word of encouragement comes from Proverbs 3:5-6, *"Trust in the Lord with all thine heart; and lean not unto thine own understanding. In all thy ways acknowledge him, and he shall direct thy paths."* In other words, trust God for your mate. Don't try to override Him. He's infinite and all wise.

Grace forgives and mercy comes with a package of love, compassion and kindness. Had it not been for God loving me, and his mercies, I don't know where I would be today. So many times I was angry with God and felt like He did not love me. During those angry moments, God did not turn his back on me. He forgave and loved me with an everlasting love. Jeremiah 31:34b states, *"I will forgive their iniquity, and I will remember their sin no more.*" Then, Jeremiah 31:3 confirms God's deep love for me: "*The Lord hath appeared of old unto me, saying, Yea, I have loved thee with an everlasting love: therefore with loving kindness have I drawn thee.*" It was meaningless to understand how a kind and loving God could love me when, at the time, I did not know how to love myself. Why did God allow me to go through those tragic moments? Today I understand. It was for this second, this minute and this hour—to be a blessing to you. Had not I lived through that pain, there would be no *Letters of Encouragement*. Psalm 111:4a tells us, "*The Lord is gracious and full of compassion.*"

Friends, no one can love you like God loves you. His love is superior to all. No one can forgive like God, whose love is immutable. There is nothing you can do that would ever make God stop loving you. He loves us even when we're in our mess. He hates sin, but He loves the sinner. I John 1:9 encourages us: "*If we confess our sins, he is faithful and just to forgive us our sins, and to cleanse us from all unrighteousness.*" Now, why would you not love a God of this magnitude?

We were created to love and worship God, not with our lips but from the heart. Jesus states the great commandment: "*Jesus said unto him, Thou shalt love the Lord thy God with all thy heart, and with all thy soul, and with all thy mind.*" (Matthew 22:37)

True love originates from God, and true worship comes from the heart. Isaiah 29:13 says, "*Wherefore the Lord said, Forasmuch as this people draw near me with their mouth, and with their lips do honor me, but have removed their heart far from me, and their fear toward me is taught by the percept of men.*"

Friends, let's be thankful for God's love and mercy. Psalm 103:8-12 declares, "*The Lord is merciful and gracious, slow to anger, and plenteous in mercy. He will not always chide:*

neither will he keep his anger for ever. He hath not dealt with us after our sins; nor rewarded us according to our iniquities. For as the heaven is high above the earth, so great is his mercy toward them that fear him. As far as the east is from the west, so far hath he removed our transgressions from us."

In closing, let us all bless the Lord in love from our hearts as we sing, *"Bless the Lord, O my soul, and forget not all his benefits: Who forgiveth all thine iniquities; who healeth all thy diseases; Who redeemeth thy life from destruction; who crowneth thee with loving-kindness and tender mercies: Who satisfieth thy mouth with good things; so that thy youth is renewed like the eagle's."* (Psalm 103:2-5)

Letter Eleven

The Separation—Heaven or Hell Which for You?

"I am he that liveth, and was dead; and, behold, I am alive for evermore, Amen; and have the keys of hell and of death."
Revelations 1:18

The Separation—Heaven or Hell Which for You?

To you my wonderful friends, what I am about to discuss with you may not be one of your favorite subjects. You may not want to continue reading after a point. I am asking you to hear what I am about to say before closing your mind. I have a few thoughts I'd like to share with you. Hopefully, at the end of this letter, you will have a different train of thought—if you are a non-believer of Hell.

If I could write whatever I wanted, or if I was allowed to do things my very own way, I would rather write a letter to your satisfaction. To write you, particularly on a subject such as Hell, grieves my heart. This is not a judgmental letter. This is a letter of biblical facts wherein the word of God does the judging. When you have been given an assignment that is driven by mandate, divine direction, choice is not an option.

Growing up, I rarely heard the word Hell mentioned. Many said, do not read the book of Revelation, it is a frightening book. Today, I love Revelation because I have come to understand what Christ has in store for me at the end of my Christian journey.

Some believe that life is to be lived in any fashion and to the fullest, thinking it can be lived without consequence after death. However, we will not escape the wrath of God without total repentance for this life on earth. Psalm 66:18 says, *"If I regard iniquity in my heart, the Lord will not hear me."* So, my dear friends, this will be the consequence of living life our way.

Think for a moment. If life were that free, there would be chaos. Imagine life without law, order and justice. There would be no care for schools, churches, law enforcement, criminal justice, politics, etc. We would hurt and take advantage of each other without any knowledge of the damage we have done. I can't even imagine a life of overwhelming disorder—it would run me insane!

I have no doubt that there are some who believe there is no such thing as Hell. Today, however, we're going to walk through several scripture readings that assert both Heaven and Hell in their fullness.

I believe in the infallible word of God. I also believe that Hell is real. I am not trying to brainwash you into believing just because I do. Nothing can be compared to experiencing something for oneself. Examine the scriptures for yourself. Then pause for a moment and think, do I believe that Hell exists? Is Hell real or is it just a myth?

Many have written books on their personal dreams, visions and hellacious experiences of God giving them a glimpse of Hell and Heaven. The Bible specifically states that judgment follows death. Hebrews 9:27 tells us, *"And as it is appointed unto men once to die, but after this the judgment."* In other words, you and I will give an account to God for the life we lived and we will be judged. Judgment is like depositing money into a savings account. Your return on asset is interest received. So it is with God: we will be rewarded for a life of godliness.

We are warned in Jude that God is coming back to execute judgment. Jude 15 says, *"To execute judgment upon all, and to convince all that are ungodly among them of all their ungodly deeds which they have ungodly committed, and of all their hard speeches which ungodly sinners have spoken against him."*

There will be no attorney to plead your case when you stand in the presence of a holy and righteous God. You will not have the opportunity to claim that you never heard the gospel or that no one ever mentioned the word Hell to you. This letter is your witness—God knows and sees all things, according to Psalm 139:1-2: *"O Lord, thou hast searched me, and known me. Thou knowest my downsitting and mine uprising, thou understandest my thought afar off."* Then, Psalm 139:7 says, *"Whither shall I go from thy spirit? or whither shall I flee from thy presence?"*

Before the return of Christ, everyone will have heard the word of God; either from the disciples themselves, through actual reading of the Bible or, in today's world, through vast media exposure. In Matthew 24:14, Jesus declares, *"And this gospel of the kingdom shall be preached in all the world for a witness unto all nations; and then shall the end come."*

God is supreme over all. Only the holy and righteous shall see God in Heaven. Isaiah 5:16 says, *"But the Lord of hosts shall be exalted in judgment, and God that is holy shall be sanctified in righteousness."*

For those that will go down to Hell, it will be a sad day. And, for those who enter Heaven, it will be a day of rejoicing. Jesus gives parables of the separation: wheat and tares. In the spiritual realm, wheat is the saved and tares are the unsaved. Jesus says in Matthew 13:40-43, *"As therefore the tares are gathered and burned in the fire; so shall it be in the end of this world. The Son of man shall send forth his angels, and they shall gather out of his kingdom all things that offend, and them which do iniquity; And shall cast them* into a furnace of fire: there shall be wailing and gnashing of teeth. Then shall the righteous shine forth as the sun in the kingdom of their Father, who hath ears to hear, let him hear."* Friends, I am working hard to remain in the wheat family.

The bible pronounces woes on the faithless. Isaiah 5:11-14 reminds us, *"Woe unto them that rise up early in the morning, that they may follow strong drink; that continue until night, till wine inflame them! And the harp, and the viol, the tabret, and pipe, and wine, are in their feasts: but they regard not the work of the Lord, neither consider the operations of his hands. Therefore my people are gone into captivity, because they have no knowledge: and their honorable men are famished, and their multitude dried up with thirst. Therefore hell hath enlarged herself, and opened her mouth without measure: and their glory, and their multitude, and their pomp, and he that rejoiceth, shall descend into it."*

Wherever your final judgment destination is, there will be no ESCAPE or CROSSOVER from Hell to Heaven. According to Luke 16:26: *"And beside all this, between us and you there is a great gulf fixed; so that they which would pass from hence to you cannot; neither can they pass to us, that would come from thence."*

The trip to Heaven or Hell is a one-way ticket—no refunds or exchanges. It will be too late to return to earth to tell your friends and loved ones that Hell is real. In Luke 16, Jesus gives a parable of a rich man and a poor man. The poor man, Lazarus, went to Heaven (Luke 16:22), and the rich man went to Hell (Luke 16:23). The rich man asked Abraham to send a warning to his brothers. Scripture tells us in Luke 16:27-28, *"Then he said, I pray thee therefore, father, that thou wouldest send him to my father's house: For I have five brethren; that he may testify unto them, lest they also come into this place of torment."* Then, in Luke 16:29-31, Abraham replies to the rich man: *"Abraham saith unto him, They have Moses and the prophets; let them hear them. And he said, Nay, father Abraham: but if one went unto them from the dead, they will repent. And he said unto him, If they hear not Moses and the prophets, neither will they be persuaded, though one rose from the dead."* Luke confirms, there will be no courier or messenger service once you have entered Hell.

Scripture confirms that Hell is a hot place. Luke 16:24 says, *"And he cried and said, Father Abraham, have mercy on me, and send Lazarus, that he may dip the tip of his finger in water, and cool my tongue; for I am tormented in this flame."* Friends, imagine Hell in your spiritual mind: screaming, hollering, begging, pleading for mercy, and finally desiring a cup of cold ice water to cool your tormented soul.

You cannot reject the Lord Jesus Christ and expect Heaven to be your home. Confession and a repentant heart are mandatory. Romans 10:9 says, *"That if thou shalt confess with thy mouth the Lord Jesus, and shalt believe in thine heart that God hath raised him from the dead, thou salt be saved. For with the heart man believeth unto righteousness; and with the mouth confession is made unto salvation."* After the sinner's prayer, begin to love God and your neighbor. Luke 10:27a says, *"Thou shalt love the Lord thy God with all thy heart, and with all thy soul, and with all thy strength, and with all thy mind, and thy neighbor as thyself."*

Now that you have confessed and repented, there should be a turning away from the old sinful life. You are now saved and have taken on the life of Christ. The word of God validates your newness in Christ. 2 Corinthians 5:17 says, *"Therefore if any man be in Christ, he is a new creature: old things are passed away; behold all things are become new."* And now that you are saved, stay saved! Do not return to the things, people and places that God has delivered you from. Proverbs 26:11 describes one who has turned back: *"As a dog returneth to his vomit, so a fool returneth to his folly."*

2 Peter 2 presents an even greater warning to the consequences of backsliding. 2 Peter 2:20-22 says, *"For if after they have escaped the pollutions of the world through the knowledge of the Lord and Savior Jesus Christ, they are again entangled therein, and overcome, the latter end is worse with them than the beginning. For it had been better for them not to have known the way of righteousness, than, after they have known it, to turn from the holy commandment delivered unto them. But it is happened unto them according to the true proverb, the dog is turned to his own vomit again; and the sow that was washed to her wallowing in the mire."*

In all that is said about Hell, we are to love God and not fear Him. He is a loving God, but He can be a God of wrath if we reject Him. God loves you unconditionally. I John 4:7 says, *"Beloved, let us love one another: for love is of God; and every one that loveth is born of God, and knoweth God."* Then, I John 4:13 says, *"Hereby know we that we dwell in him, and he in us, because he hath given us of his Spirit."*

Friends, it's time to cross over to Heaven, the good place, to a taste of honey, a land filled with milk. Psalm 34:8 says, *"O taste and see that the Lord is good."*

In the book of Revelation, John was given revelations of things to come to pass in the future. God gave the revelation to Jesus Christ, His Son, to be shown to John by means of an angel (messenger) in Revelation 1:1-3.

According to Revelation, God is keeping record of how we have lived our lives. God has a book called the book of life, and we will be judged from this book. All those that did not make it into heaven will be cast into the lake of fire. John says in Revelation 20:12, *"And I saw the dead, small and great, stand before God; and the books were opened: and another book was opened, which is the book of life: and the dead were judged out of those things which were written in the books, according to their works."* Then, Revelation

20:15 says, *"And whosoever was not found written in the book of life was cast into the lake of fire."*

God showed John visions of many. John saw the new heaven and the new earth. Revelation 21:1-2 says, *"And I saw a new heaven and a new earth: for the first heaven and the first earth were passed away; and there was no more sea. And I John saw the holy city, new Jerusalem, coming down from God out of heaven, prepared as a bride adorned for her husband."*

Friends, in Heaven we will be free of pain, sickness and sorrow. According to Revelation 21:4, *"And God shall wipe away all tears from their eyes; and there shall be no more death, neither sorrow, nor crying, neither shall there be any more pain: for the former things are passed away."* Amen to pain for me!

Those in Heaven will praise God. Revelation 19:1 says, *"And after these things I heard a great voice of much people in heaven, saying, Alleluia; Salvation, and glory, and honor, and power, unto the Lord our God."*

The return of Christ will be the marriage supper of the lamb, according to Revelation 19:7: *"Let us be glad and rejoice, and give honor to him: for the marriage of the Lamb is come, and his wife hath made herself ready."*

When will Christ return? The bible records that no man knows the day and hour. Jesus does give signs before the end, as we see in Matthew 24:36: *"But of that day and hour knoweth no man, no, not the angels of heaven, but my Father only."* Friends, be careful. Some have already calculated the time of Jesus's return although the bible clearly says "no man knoweth." Let no one deceive you, read the word for yourself. Matthew 24:42-44 cautions that Christ returns as a thief: *"Watch therefore: for ye know not what hour your Lord doth come. But know this, that if the goodman of the house had known in what watch the thief would come, he would have watched, and would not have suffered his house to be broken up. Therefore be ye also ready: for in such an hour as ye think not the Son of man cometh.*"

Signs before the end: Jesus says in Matthew 24:5-8, "*For many shall come in my name, saying, I am Christ; and shall deceive many. And ye shall hear of wars and rumors of wars: see that ye be not troubled: for all these things must come to pass, but the end is not yet. For nation shall rise against nation, and kingdom against kingdom: and there shall be famines, and pestilences, and earthquakes, in divers places. All these are the begging of sorrows.*" Then, Matthew 24:14 states, "*And this gospel of the kingdom shall be preached in all the world for a witness unto all nations; and then shall the end come.*" Friends, reading this passage from scripture reaffirms what was stated earlier: excuses that you have never heard the scriptures will not be accepted.

I wonder what Heaven looks like? According to Revelation Chapter 21, God carried John away in the spirit and showed him the new Jerusalem and its beauty. Revelation 21:10-14 says, "*And he carried me away in the spirit to a great and high mountain, and showed me that great city, the holy Jerusalem, descending out of heaven from God, Having the glory of God: and her light was like unto a stone most precious, even like a jasper stone, clear as crystal; And had a wall great and high, and had twelve gates, and at the gates twelve angels, and names written thereon, which are the names of the twelve tribes of the children of Israel; On the east three gates; on the north three gates; on the south three gates, and on the west three gates.*"

May I share with you the beauty of Heaven as described in the bible? Revelation 21:21 tells us, "*And the twelve gates were twelve pearls: every several gate was of one pearl: and the street of the city was pure gold, as it were transparent glass.*" Hallelujah, Praise God!

How will Christ return? I Thessalonians 4:16-18 says, "*For the Lord himself shall descend from heaven with a shout, with the voice of the archangel, and with the trump of God: and the dead in Christ shall rise first: Then we which are alive and remain shall be caught up together with them in the clouds, to meet the Lord in the air: and so shall we ever be with the Lord."*

Upon Christ's return it will be too late to start preparing—your spiritual house must be in order. Revelation 22:10-11 says, *"And he saith unto me, Seal not the sayings of the prophecy of this book: for the time is at hand. He that is unjust, let him be unjust still: and he which is filthy, let him be filthy still: and he that is righteous, let him be righteous still: and he that is holy, let him be holy still."*

God is coming quickly with His reward in His hand to pay everyone according to the lives we have lead. Revelation 22:12 says, *"And, behold, I come quickly; and my reward is with me, to give every man according as his work shall be."*

Friends, on that final day the unsaved will go into everlasting punishment (Hell) and the righteous into life eternal (Heaven). Matthew 25:46 confirms, *"And these shall go away into everlasting punishment: but the righteous into life eternal."* In closing I want to leave you with a question? Will you be ready on that great and wonderful day of the coming of the Lord?

Letter Twelve

Thank You, God

"In every thing give thanks: for this is the will of God in Christ Jesus concerning you."
I Thessalonians 5:18

Letter Twelve

Thank You, God

T hank you, God, for the many and wonderful blessings you have bestowed upon me. What I am—you have made me. Where I am today—it is you, Father, who has brought me here. And I say, thank you, thank you, Father Lord Jesus! My heart is overwhelmed in you.

Father, you were merciful unto me. Psalm 103:8 says, *"The LORD is merciful and gracious, slow to anger, and plenteous in mercy."* Father, all power is in your hand. You have the power to heal, destroy and defend. You defended me, Lord Jesus. Father, time after time I was so frustrated, discouraged and angry. I knew that I was living to the best of your word, and yet I was suffering day and night beyond any relief. Father, you were working behind the scene and I am truly grateful. Father, you were preparing me for this day— *Letters of Encouragement.* Father, your word tells us, *"This is the day which the LORD hath made; we will rejoice and be glad in it."* (Psalm 118:24) Father, you could have consumed me in my anger. For anger, you gave me love. Father, your word says, *"It is of the LORD's mercies that we are not consumed, because his compassions fail not. They are new every morning: great is thy faithfulness."* (Lamentations 3:22-23)

Father, you saw my afflictions and you delivered me out of them. Psalm 107:19-20 tells us, *"Then they cry unto the LORD in their trouble, and he saveth them out of their distresses. He sent his word, and healed them, and delivered them from their destructions."* Father, each time I felt as though I wanted to give up, you sent a word of encouragement. Thank you.

Father, my desire is to be Christ like. Philippians 2:5 says, *"Let this mind be in you, which was also in Christ Jesus."* Father, without your mind, I can do nothing. Lord Jesus, in Philippians 4:13, your word says, *"I can do all things through Christ which strengtheneth me."* Father, you gave me strength to bring *Letters of Encouragement* to completion. Thank you, Father.

Father, I am reaching for higher heights and deeper depths in you. Philippians 3:14 says, *"I press toward the mark for the prize of the high calling of God in Christ Jesus."* Father, I rejoice in you. Philippians 4:4 says, *"Rejoice in the LORD always: and again I say, Rejoice."*

Father, as I close out *Letters of Encouragement* I ask that you would touch and change the heart of one that is hurting in despair as I was. Lord, give them a new life—make them a vessel of honor unto you. Lord, your word says, *"If a man therefore purge himself from these, he shall be a vessel unto honor, sanctified, and meet for the master's use, and prepared unto every good work."* (2 Timothy 2:21)

Lord Jesus, set them free from the life of bondage that is keeping them from surrendering and being free in you. Father, give them the strength to walk away from the life that may possibly destroy them. Father, help them to endure. 2 Timothy 2:3 says, *"Thou therefore endure hardness, as a good soldier of Jesus Christ."*

Father, reveal yourself to them in a supernatural way. Father, deliver them from the yoke of bondage. Isaiah says in Isaiah 14:3, *"And it shall come to pass in the day that the LORD shall give thee rest from thy sorrow, and from thy fear, and from the hard bondage wherein thou wast made to serve."*

Father let them know that, once they have surrendered their lives to you, your word will set them free. Romans 8:1 says, *"There is therefore now no condemnation to them which are in Christ Jesus, who walk not after the flesh, but after the Spirit."*

Thank you, Lord Jesus. You are a prayer-answering God. To you, my wonderful readers, I pray that God answers your prayers, that your souls have been revived and your spirit strengthened.

In Gratitude to Those Who Have Touched My Life

Tammy Fraley, Masood Basha, Rhonda Stevens, Jon Witherow, Rosalind Mood, Krystal Granville, Isaiah D. Newman, Jr., Onyx Granville, Kellie Copeland-Burnup, Sherri Timmermann, Carol Reid and Patricia Hill—all of you were God sent. It would have been impossible for me to bring *Letters of Encouragement* to completion without your patience and tireless dedication to this project. I am grateful to the Most High God for your love, loyalty and commitment. You are true friends, and I love you very much. Thank you from the bottom of my heart.

Arlene, Jerry and Amber Vereen, Natalie and Landon Davis—my cheerleaders—you rallied me on to the very end. Thank you for your love, support and encouragement.

Gloria Louise Gillison—thank you for your friendship and inspiration. You are an awesome woman of God. We did not meet by accident. It was the providential arrangement of God. I am truly blessed by your music during the rough times.

Special appreciation goes to Pastor Joe L. Brown, Mother Laura Brown and Pastor Mary Jo Young; Pastor William A. Prioleau, Evangelist Ena Prioleau, Deacon Joseph Scott and Evening of Prayer COGIC; Reverend Isaac and Mrs. Jannie

Holt, First Lady Natasha, Aunt Betty and Latica; Giffin, Andy, Giff and Lisa Daughtridge; George Billings, Jay and Annette Wein, Kristin Shuey, Paula and Jeff Jones, John and Nicole Bernier, Jeff Powers, Danielle Powers, Jessica Robinson, Virgil Simmons, Eddie Joe, Donna Thomas, Chris Gasser and Steve Spires; Melody Lewis and Princetta Johnson; Raphael, Sarene, Jaydn, Grant and Nia James; Dan DiMicco, John Ferriola, Ladd and Sally Hall, Yvette Camille, Andrew Fletcher, Suchi Jain, Susie Richardson, Lisa Darling, Mark Harold, Harold Flowers, Roddy Marraccini, Eric McGuire, Jason Christman, Randy Krause, Rick Blume and Queen Jetta Nicole; Meleah and Darin Reynolds, Linda Starr, and Frances Chesnut; Shaunda Hall, Mark Bennett, Gary Schmaltz, Ed and Joyce Bailey, Pete Kroeger, Robert Derosiers, Lori Johansmeyer, Isiah Lebird, Franz Sainvil, Charles Perkins and Raul Alarcon; David and Greta Brown, Holly Kirkpatrick, Donna King, Melinda Morgan, Marty Jones, Sadie Beach, Janice Smith, Evondra Pinckney, Patricia Strong, Denise Scott, LeighR Slates, Kelley Shaw, Daphne Davis, Buffy Fortner, Sheri Pearson, Mr. WT and Crystalyn Watford. My love to all of you!

CPSIA information can be obtained at www.ICGtesting.com
Printed in the USA
LVOW061938221211

260762LV00002B/1/P